More praise for *Among Grizzlies*

"Treadwell's descriptions of bears and bear behavior is a delightful tale that animal lovers will enjoy."

—*Naples News* (FL)

"Captivating . . . A lively and sometimes humorous narration . . . His writing is so very vivid you almost believe you were there. . . . Treadwell has found a purpose in his life, and he shares it fervently, wittily."

—Carolyn Spector
KLCC, National Public Radio

"Amazing . . . A delightful combination of science and spirit."

—*Everett Herald* (WA)

"Remarkable . . . An inspiring story of recovery . . . A treat for readers of any age."

—*Publishers Weekly* (starred review)

AMONG GRIZZLIES

LIVING WITH WILD BEARS
IN ALASKA

Timothy Treadwell
and Jewel Palovak

Ballantine Books • New York

To Ted Endicott,
for your heart, home,
and belief in us.

2005 Ballantine Books Trade Paperback Edition

Copyright © 1997 by Timothy Treadwell and Jewel Palovak

All rights reserved.

Published in the United States by Ballantine Books, an imprint of The Random
House Publishing Group, a division of Random House, Inc., New York.

BALLANTINE and colophon are registered trademarks of Random House, Inc.

Originally published in hardcover in the United States
by HarperCollins Publishers, in 1997.

This edition published by arrangement with HarperCollins Publishers, Inc.

ISBN 0-345-42605-3

Cover design: Cathy Colbert
Cover photograph: Timothy Treadwell

www.ballantinebooks.com

Introduction

For thirteen summers, armed with only a camera, Timothy Treadwell traveled to the wilds of Alaska on a mission to protect grizzly bears. In October of 2003, Timothy died in the field among the bears he devoted his life to. During his expeditions, Timothy respectfully recorded many generations of grizzly bears, while his presence along the Alaska coast protected them from poachers. Each year when he returned to civilization, he would craft his images into an educational campaign, reaching over ten thousand people throughout North America, exposing them to the secret world of the grizzly bear.

He was the founder of Grizzly People, a grassroots organization devoted to preserving bears and their wilderness habitat. Grizzly People's mission is to elevate the grizzly to the kindred state of the whale and the dolphin through supportive education in the hopes that humans will learn to live in peace with the bear, wilderness, and fellow humans.

Grizzly People's main goals are protection and education. During 2003, Timothy's last summer in Alaska, he documented what park officials admit appears to be an abandoned hunting camp in the middle of Katmai National Park. In 2004, the first summer without Timothy's presence, six bears were poached in the park. Grizzly People will continue Timothy's quest to battle poaching, increased bear hunting, and grizzly bear delisting.

Education goes hand and hand with protection and preservation, since it is education that stirs people to act. Grizzly People will turn Timothy's images into multi-media presentations for the public and for organizations working toward bear preservation.

Timothy Treadwell was an adventurer who lived life to the fullest. He was a preservationist, an educator, and a friend to all species. He had a passion to share the beauty of wild animals, living wild lives in wild places. In his spirit, Grizzly People will continue Timothy's work, inspiring humans to be great stewards of our planet

Jewel Palovak
Grizzly People
April 2005

Scientific Credits

Much of the scientific information in this book about bears has been taught to me by a variety of bear scholars. They include Dr. James Halfpenny of Colorado State, Dr. Barrie Gilbert of Utah State, and Dr. Stephen Herrero of the University of Calgary. For many years I have also been fortunate enough to have the guidance of world-renowned biologist Larry Aumiller of the Alaska Department of Fish and Game. Information pertaining to poaching and the trade of bear parts has been provided by my friend Keith Highley, an independent wildlife trade and fisheries researcher. The finished information was reviewed by David Mattson at the University of Idaho. I am extremely thankful for their guidance and expertise. However, they are not responsible for any errors I may have made in the interpretation of scientific facts for this book.

1

Within the last wild lands of North America dwells an animal that inspires respect and fear around the world. It is the grizzly bear, a living legend of the wilderness. Grizzlies can sprint thirty-five plus miles an hour, smell carrion at nine or more miles, and drag a thousand-pound animal up steep mountains. The grizzly bear is one of a very few animals remaining on earth that can kill a human in physical combat. It can decapitate with a single swipe, or grotesquely disfigure a person in rapid order. Within the last wilderness areas where they dwell, they are the undisputed king of all beasts. I know this all very well. My name is Timothy Treadwell, and I live with the wild grizzly.

The path that led me to the land of the grizzly was far more dangerous than the bears themselves. I was the third of five children, raised in New York State. My parents loved me and did the best they could, but I was a handful. I wasn't a criminal kid, just a bit mischievous, with the heart of a wild animal.

Since I was very young, animals have meant a great deal to me. As a child, I donned imaginary wings, claws, and fangs. To me, animals possessed the innocence and freedom that I could only wish for. My childhood was haunted by fantasies of riding away on a wild horse, or running far and fast with a pack of timber wolves. I daydreamed throughout my school years. Sometimes I rocketed into outer space, exploring other worlds. Other times I cruised the Old West with my best friends, Butch Cassidy and the Sundance Kid. In my head I became a grizzly, roaming the great north, or a Bengal tiger in the lush jungles of Asia. I always came out of my fantasy world just enough to pass all of my classes. Actually, I got above average grades. My buddy Butch Cassidy knew algebra and biology.

As a young boy, an incident occurred that would change my life forever. One day at a pond, my friend Ricky and I happened on some older kids who were throwing frogs high into the air and splattering them on the muddy water's surface. They had a bucket full of the hapless little creatures, and one by one, they were murdering them. I tried to rescue the frogs, but the two boys were not only older than I was, they were tougher. They tossed me into the reeds like a rag doll. Ricky tried to help, but was quickly pummeled and ran off crying with a face full of dirt. Thinking they were rid of us, the thugs continued their executions. But I was determined to set the frogs free. Crawling out of the weeds, I found a long wooden plank and sneaked up on the punks. I smacked one from behind, and hit the other full in the face with the board. I ran them off, swinging wildly at their backs. Then I liberated the frogs. An eco-warrior was born.

As I became a teenager, my home life disintegrated. Especially after I got stinking drunk, smashed up the family car, and was arrested. Bingeing on beer and Tom Collinses became my preferred pastime, and my studies were all but forgotten. After just barely graduating from high school, I left home. In my chaotic state, abandoning my family was the best gift I could give them.

I landed in Long Beach, California, an overactive street punk without any skills, prospects, or hopes. What little assets and attributes I possessed were quickly devoured by a voracious drinking problem. Alcohol soon gave way to drugs. If alcohol was slowly consuming my soul, drugs would quickly incinerate it. My downward spiral continued on life's darker side. I medicated myself with lines of cocaine, buckets of booze, and sprinkled in the new thrills of crystal meth and Quaaludes. Incidents of madness and danger occurred with frightening frequency.

One evening I was invited to a private party by some low-life drug dealers. One of the scumbags, Turk, was constantly putting me down and intimidating me.

"You're one of those maggot hanger-on types, ain't ya, Treadwell?" said Turk while chopping lines of glittering snowy powder. "You'd probably blow us all for our coke!"

"Fuck you, Turk," I snapped back.

"You'd love to, wouldn't you, faggot boy?" said Turk.

I was standing over Turk in the dining room, where he sat hunched at the head of the table, when a rage came over me. I kicked my tennis shoe into Turk's smug face, knocking him backward into an expensive antique hutch. Fine china avalanched to the ground, some cracking over Turk's bloody mug. The other three dope dealers lit into me. None of them was much bigger than me, but they were tougher than nails. They punched and slapped at me, then flung me headfirst into a wall. Curiously, my head went through the wall, and I was suddenly gazing into the kitchen. Dazed, I looked around, momentarily awed by the shiny, well-appointed room. Meanwhile, the dopers were still in the dining room with the rest of my body, kicking and striking me with abandon. Growling, I extricated my torso from the kitchen, grabbed a heavy wooden chair, and began spinning around like a top. Different parts of the chair smacked the guys on the heads and shoulders, and sent them crashing into the furniture. The dining table flipped over, flinging several hundred dollars' worth of cocaine and a bevy of half-drunk cocktails to the hardwood floor. I caught a large, pricey chandelier with one leg of the chair, and a fireworks explosion of glass and sparkling, shattered lightbulbs flew through the air. The battered drug dealers lay on the ground or against stained walls. Then one grabbed a .357 magnum. The moment I spied that, I retreated out the front door, across the manicured lawn, and into the quiet streets. Randy, the one with the gun, pursued me, quickly cocking the weapon. My knee was battered, and the pain slowed me down. Randy cornered me, and with both hands pointed the gun at my head.

"Kill me, motherfucker!" I screamed. "Enjoy your life in prison!"

Neighborhood lights were blinking on. Randy placed the gun in his waistband.

"Fucking Treadwell," he said. Shaking his head, he walked away.

In the weeks that followed, I sank lower and lower, living in a paranoid, spooky, surreal nightmare. I armed myself, walking in public with a Ruger 9-millimeter pistol concealed in the waistband of my trousers. At night I slept with a locked and loaded M-16. I was fearless, dangerous, and vicious. Instinct told me to leave this life behind, but instead of running away, I stayed chained to my path of self-destruction.

One evening, when I had drunk more beer than usual, I needed some drugs to level me out. In my world there were many dealers to choose from.

I decided to go to Rick and Dennis's house to get some cocaine. In the center of the living room stood a massive wooden table surrounded by cushy sofas. Heavy-metal music vibrated through the room. On the table lay lines of cocaine and balloons full of heroin.

"Man, where have you been?" asked Rick. "You're a mess! Come on, Tim, take a load off," he said, patting the seat next to him.

Dennis sat me down on one of the plush sofas and skillfully etched two thick lines on a mirror. The first was a familiar glittering granular column of gorgeous cocaine. The second, an alien mud-colored row. The brown stuff, Dennis explained, was kick-ass Mexican heroin. I snorted each vigorously, utilizing separate nostrils as Dennis beamed like a proud parent. Next, he sprinkled a bunch of the brown heroin on a piece of aluminum foil and lit the bottom. As the powder liquefied, he showed me how to inhale the raspy fumes. I repeated these activities a few times, eager to catch a new kind of buzz. Yet I didn't feel the promised heavenly highs of the drugs. Instead, something felt very wrong. Calmly, I asked Rick to step outside. My intoxication began to mutate, and whatever instinct of survival remained, it had Timothy Treadwell's full attention.

"Rick, I'm really sorry, but I'm feeling worse than sick," I whispered, watching his form shift and sway in front of me. "I think that maybe I ought to go to a hospital."

Now I'd pissed him off. "Treadwell, don't ruin my fucking night!" he spat at me. "We don't need this. Just get the hell home and sleep it off. You are such a pain in the ass!" he snapped, slamming the door in my face.

I started to stumble home, trying to take Rick's advice. But I couldn't quite make it. Gathering the last of my strength, I headed for Terry Tabor's house.

Terry was a good friend who had served two tours of duty in Vietnam. The military spirit was still with him, for he spoke in the clipped tones of an army sergeant.

"Treadwell, you're a good guy with your whole life ahead of you," Terry often told me. "Don't screw it up because of dope. You have too much to contribute to this world, soldier." I loved that Terry Tabor and often wished I could follow his advice.

Terry Tabor knew death all too well. His two tours of duty in Vietnam had been nightmares of carnage and dissolution. Terry

Tabor knew all about drug overdoses, too. They had occurred in Vietnam, and here in his postwar world. Terry took one look at me and woke his girlfriend.

"Chrissy, fire up the van on the double!" he ordered. "We gotta move out and get Timmy to the hospital or we're going to lose him!"

I was vomiting on the front lawn, my head spinning out of control as they loaded me into the van. As Chrissy sped down the street, I finally felt the serene effects of the heroin. Not the highs that Rick and Dennis were chasing, simply the numbing sensation of incoming death.

Suddenly, a weight crushed my chest. Terry Tabor had me on the floor of the van and was using CPR, struggling to keep my heart beating. I was barely conscious as they rushed me into the ER, faces and noises swimming above my head. I was wheeled into the trauma unit, where frantic interns slapped a defibrillator to my chest and blasted my heart back to a beat. Once I was out of the woods, they hooked me up to an IV just to keep me stable after the overdose. Terry Tabor had saved my miserable life.

That close call with the grim reaper forced me to evaluate my status on earth. Timothy Treadwell was a minimum-wage-earning, name-tag-toting loser crippled by multiple poisonous addictions. I had nothing to contribute to society and no real future. Part of me had died during my ordeal, and another part of me wished I was dead. Yet something kept me clinging to a faint sense of hope. I remembered my desire as a child to ride away on a wild horse, or run far and fast with a pack of wolves. Somewhere, someplace, beyond the honk of horns and burning glare of city lights, was sanctuary. My sanctuary. With little more than a worthless life to lose, I had to find it or die trying.

I sought the counsel of my hero and friend Terry Tabor, hoping that he could give me some direction.

"OK, soldier," Terry drilled, "what is the main objective of your operation?"

"Terry, I've got to get out of here," I exclaimed. "I need to be somewhere really remote, far away from people."

"Alrighty, then, you've got half a plan. What would you like to see, where do you want to travel?" Terry asked.

"Somewhere beautiful, Terry. Somewhere with mountains, rivers, and cascading waterfalls. Most of all, somewhere where there aren't many people. I want to see animals. Lots of wild animals," I replied.

"Affirmative, son! Now your plan's starting to take shape! If you had your wish, what animal would you most like to see?" Terry inquired.

"Well, this might seem crazy, but when I was young I used to pretend I was a grizzly bear. I've always wanted to see bears, Terry," I said.

"Now there's an animal that could really kick some ass! Clean yourself up, Treadwell, get some cheap transportation, and get yourself out of here. If it's open land and wild animals that you want, there's no doubt about it, Alaska is the answer. Fucking-A right, soldier, Alaska!"

2

Nearly a year after Terry Tabor proclaimed Alaska as my goal, I was at last ready to hit the road. With money saved, a dependable motorcycle, and endless hours of research about Alaska under my belt, I was prepared for a summer journey that would take me across fifteen thousand miles of road, four U.S. states, and three Canadian provinces, into the land of the grizzly bear.

After thousands of miles of driving, I was in America's largest national park, Wrangell-St. Elias. While hiking alone along the banks of the raging Chitina River, I had my first encounter with a bear. The Chitina (pronounced CHIT-na) flows raucously northwest to the Copper River, and then spirits off to the sea. The river is nourished by the melting ice of a multitude of glaciers, among them the Logan, Walsh, Baldwin, and Chitina Glacier itself. As the water raged past with a deafening roar, on its bank a row of thick vegetation and shrubbery next to me began to rustle and then sway violently. I froze in my muddy tracks, eyes bulging as I watched the brush. I broke out in a cold sweat as the weeds thrashed and an enormous fur-clad animal bounded out onto the path. A grizzly! My mouth dropped open in astonishment as the animal and I locked gazes. Its nostrils flared, inhaling deep puffs of my scent through a black-tipped snout. The bear's jaw slowly unhinged, revealing rows of powerful sharp yellow teeth. Given the chance, I would have been afraid, yet in that moment of mutual recognition, the bear pivoted on its back paws and bolted in a violent retreat. It was the briefest of encounters, the first time that I stood near a truly wild beast. My heart was pounding and I was shaken, both equally elated and saddened by the meeting. Elated, for it was my dream come true to meet a bear in the wilderness. Sad, because as imposing as the bear was, it was afraid of me. In the wilderness, this bear should be frightened of nothing. Yet a brief glimpse of a human had caused it to flee. The message was clear to me. After decades of adversity caused by man, the bear was wary of people. For me, the encounter was like looking into a mirror. I gazed into the face of a kindred soul, a being that was potentially lethal, but in reality was just as frightened as I was.

A few weeks later I booked a seat aboard a float plane to a remote region of western Alaska. The area was noted for two species: sockeye salmon and brown grizzly bears. The mass spawning cycle of the salmon enticed hungry predators, like the grizzly and human sport fishermen. I came in peace, hoping to perhaps view a wild bear, and maybe actually photograph one.

From the Cessna 208, the view of Alaska's sweeping green landscape was amazing. The two other paying customers, both veteran fishermen, let me sit up front with the pilot so I could see as much as possible. The sky was dreary, with a canopy of high, unbroken clouds. As we buzzed aloft at about a thousand feet, I peered, craned, and swiveled in every direction to take in this big Alaska. Below were vibrant emerald plains sandwiched between huge ice-clad mountains that tore through the clouds. Periodically, the pastures were interrupted by pools of still black water and meager stands of trees. On the ground below I knew that there were animals of every sort: caribou, moose, fox, wolves, and the one animal I came so many miles to see, the grizzly bear.

We landed in a lake that seemed much more like an ocean's bay, and I chose a campsite near a gathering of fishermen. After all, I was a total beginner at wilderness camping. The campground had a fire pit and fresh water, and most important, an elevated wooden food cache to protect all edibles from marauding bears. As much of a novice as I was, I knew never to leave human food out where a wild bear could get to it. Once a bear has encountered people food, it can become a nuisance and even a potential killer.

Each day of my week in this wilderness I dutifully set out on lone hikes along the lake and creeks in search of bears. For the most part, the sport fishermen had effectively driven away all wildlife in the area. Neil, an insurance salesman from Iowa, told me of a trail several miles from camp that might be full of bears. Neil was, head to toe, an authentic fisherman. Lures hung out of his pockets, and his khaki vest was crammed with fishing paraphernalia. Flies hung off a floppy hat, glittering brightly in the daylight. The trail he spoke of was in a very wooded area that led to a river that attracted a good share of bears.

"I been fishing here every year for the last decade and only visited that place but once," Neil testified. "Well, shit! There were so many goddamned bears back there, I only needed to see it once to have enough." Neil went on, eyes bugging out in excitement, "You know, I ain't an insurance salesman for nothing. I tell ya, that place ain't good for your health. In fact, Timothy, if you're so set on going there, why don't you borrow my .44 magnum?" he offered.

"No thanks," I returned sincerely. "I could never kill a bear. Besides, this is their home, and I'm an invader. But thanks again for the tip."

I set out to find the bear path later in the afternoon. Neil and the others all agreed that, in order to avoid humans, the bears tended to come out either early in the morning or late in the day.

After eating a hearty late lunch of several peanut butter sand-wiches, I decided not to pack any food because it might attract the bears. My gear consisted of one good Minolta camera with a 100–300 lens, film, rain gear, and a few plastic trash bags to pro-tect everything from moisture. Showers were frequent in these parts of Alaska, so I had to be prepared. I walked along the lake for about an hour and finally found the trail, twisting through a forest of tall pines.

My enthusiasm waned at the sight of the path, for it was the stuff of nightmares. Huge pines lined either side of the narrow trail, forming an eerie canopy. It was beginning to rain as I stepped onto the path, a fine mist washing over my face. I was filled with terror, thoughts of my previous sighting still fresh in my mind. The one thing I wanted most was to see bears, yet I had never felt as much fear as on this lone walk through their habitat. My dread increased as I realized that this trail wasn't made by anything human, but was worn by centuries of perpetual bear use. All along the trail, the trees were raked raw of bark, no doubt by bears. Green moss hung everywhere, like massive spiderwebs. The glow-ing carpet of moss shrouded fallen trees, forms that looked like beasts lying in wait for me. All along the thick vegetation were piles of scat, or bear poop. The mounds were like wet stacks of squishy black coal, and smelled of rotting fish. All of the dump was rather fresh, justifying my bear paranoia. When I reached the bank of a river, the rain stopped. This looked like as good a place as any to stake out and await the brown inhabitants. My heart was thumping audibly, and I was literally shaking in my boots.

Hours passed, and not a single bear visited. Showers came and went. When it wasn't raining, mosquitoes dined on any exposed area of my body. Some wise-assed winged creature, a whitesocks, flew up my trouser legs and gnawed violently into my raw skin. The rain forced other bugs into hiding, but caused its own obvious misery. My flimsy rain gear left me soaking wet, struggling to keep my valuable camera equipment dry. Tears welled up in my eyes, mixing with the rain as I sat on the soggy bank. All I wanted was the company of bears.

After eleven P.M., as the long Alaska daylight ebbed, I gave up, heading back to camp through the forest trail. The path had become dark and slick with rain.

Without warning, the path ahead crackled and crunched as heavy steps padded my way. In the dim light a massive form took shape, a shape that did not look human. As the silhouette came into focus, there was no doubt that it was a bear. As the bear slowly ambled my way, fear enveloped me. My body told me to run, run as fast as I could, but my brain knew better. Without turning my back on the bear, I slowly retreated and started singing softly. What I sang, I haven't a clue, but it calmed my frazzled nerves. Maybe it communicated some goodwill to the approaching bear, because the animal veered off to my left and disappeared into the night. I shook with adrenaline spiked with fear. Triumphantly, I resumed the hike back to camp. Unlike my first encounter in the Wrangell-St. Elias, this bear did not run from me, and didn't even appear to be afraid. It was the epitome of what I had hoped for in this journey to Alaska.

Just as I began to gloat, another bear came my way. Bolstered by my previous strategy, I began to sing again, backing up with every note. This bear was huffing my way, but stopped and blinked curiously at my warbling. He reached the riverbank, and once again veered off to the left, proceeding nonchalantly up the river. I was shaken, and, frankly, I'd had enough of bears for the evening. I couldn't wait to return to Neil and the other fishermen, ready to brag about my success with the bears. I tentatively set off again for camp. I almost made it out. But almost isn't good enough in the wilderness.

A third bear confidently plodded toward me. This brown bear was massive, possibly weighing 1,000 pounds. On all fours, the bear's head was as high as mine. Again I attempted to withdraw by walking backward and singing stuttering, sweet songs, but my strategy ran into a glitch. This bear's normal walking pace was much quicker than my reverse steps. Each passing second brought the grizzly closer to me. The bear quickly closed the remaining distance between us. I stumbled on the wet mud, falling down hard, face first. As I curled into the fetal position, the grizzly's steps vibrated the ground right up to my sniveling face. Pearl-dagger claws stopped inches from my cheek. Spreading my fingers over my eyes in a bizarre form of peek-aboo, I gaped up at the grizzly's face. What little light remained exposed an immense furry face, horribly engraved with long, deep scars that told of past battles. He exhaled a puff of fish-scented breath, then quickly inhaled my odor. No brilliant defensive strategies occurred to me. I was on overload with terror, and simply seized up. The grizzly hovered above for a few minutes, but for me, down on the ground, it felt like a lifetime. Then, ever so gently, he stepped over my quivering body, his bloated tummy scraping across my right shoulder, and vanished in the direction of the river.

Long after he was gone, I picked up my shaking body and clumsily left the woods, all the while chanting, "Thank you, bears . . . thank you, bears." This brush with the wild grizzly was more than I had ever hoped for. Upon returning to camp, I told no one of the experience.

After returning to California, I enthusiastically sought out my great friend and advisor, Terry Tabor. When I arrived at his home, there was a scurry of people removing boxes and furniture. I panicked, thinking to myself that Terry had never mentioned anything about moving out. Another of Terry's friends, Chris Marshall, saw my confusion and approached me solemnly.

"Where's Terry, Chris? Where did he go?" I asked in a faltering voice.

Chris put his hand on my shoulder and got right to the point. "None of us knew it, but Terry had been sick for a very long time. His heart finally gave out, Timothy. We've lost Terry." I was crushed. There was nothing else to do but assist with the sad cleanup ritual . . . and cry.

With the passing of Terry and the trip to Alaska, powerful emotions awakened my spirit. How I wish I could have told Terry about the big grizzly that spared my life. Deep down inside, I felt that Terry did know. Terry had always believed that I could make a valuable contribution to the planet. For Terry, the big grizzly, and all other bears, I was at last willing to try.

I religiously gathered knowledge about grizzlies. I learned that over 100,000 grizzlies had once thrived in America's lower forty-eight states, and that perhaps less than 1,000 remain today. Bears of the continental United States today cling to dwindling habitats in only four states: the Greater Yellowstone ecosystem, mainly in Wyoming but also stretching into Idaho and Montana; the Northern Continental Divide, which takes in Glacier National Park and the Bob Marshall Wilderness complex, all within Montana; the Cabinet-Yakk ecosystem of northwestern Montana; the Selkirk Mountains of northern Idaho; a possible scattering of bear within the Selway-Bitterroot Wilderness of north-central Montana; and a small population in the northern Cascades of Washington State. I also learned that many bears, including grizzlies, are being illegally poached for their gallbladders, a prized ingredient in traditional Asian medicine. I was appalled to learn that grizzlies were still being sport-hunted for little more than macho thrills and trophy decorations in Alaska, Canada, and Russia. Most important, I found out that grizzly bears can only live in a complete wilderness, and that greedy developers were extinguishing these areas, leaving nothing for the precious animals.

But how could one person make a positive difference for bears? And, really, who was I kidding? Although my heroin overdose had been my last experience with drugs, I still consumed massive amounts of alcohol at home. As long as I drank, it was impossible for me to truly be a responsible defender of bears. Though I had tried to quit drinking countless times before, nothing really ever worked. Only a miracle could save me. Next year, one would come in the form of a powerful grizzly.

3

The following year I couldn't wait to return to Alaska. Careful months of research taught me more about the science of bears. The grizzlies dominate wilderness ecosystems where they live. Bears can sprint faster than a racehorse, swim great distances, and easily climb steep mountains. On open ground, bears can move at an average speed of six miles an hour for twenty-four hours without stopping for rest, food, or drink. Bears are omnivorous, eating both plants and meat. From late autumn to early spring, when the weather is cold and food is no longer abundant, they simply curl up in a den and sleep through the inhospitable period. Bears are animals in perfect balance with their natural environment.

My research had also revealed an obscure area in which grizzlies abounded. As the summer solstice arrived, I was aboard a Cessna 185 float plane, hurtling toward a new adventure in western Alaska. In this particular area of Alaska, just south of the Arctic Circle, the sun sets around midnight. Even after midnight, the sun, which hung just below the horizon, gave off an ambient luminous glow. In areas north of the Arctic Circle, the sun did not actually set from May eighth through August second. The long hours of light were perfect for my launch into the wild. It was around ten P.M., and I had been up since five A.M. that same day, waiting for a bush plane that had been delayed since early morning. I was fighting exhaustion, trying to stay alert, hoping to see bears.

After nearly an hour of flying, the plane sneaked between two enormous snow-clad mountains, then swooped down toward vast pastures of fairly open green fields. Interspersed among the fields were creeks, mud flats, and some brown cattle. What the hell were cattle doing out here in forgotten Alaska? Looking closer, I realized that I wasn't seeing livestock, but that it was a magnificent gathering of huge grizzly bears! As the pilot glided across the fields, a quiet distance above the bears, I tried to count the animals, but lost track somewhere in the sixties. A strange sensation came over me as I realized that I would be alone among a multitude of wild beasts. The pilot saw the bears, too, and became concerned for my safety. He decided that it would be too dangerous for me to sleep alone among the mass migration of bears, and he made a major tactical decision that would quickly prove disastrous. As we circled the ocean bay, he elected to drop me on the opposite side of a roaring river that would buffer my camp from the vast fields that were full of bears. Then he unloaded me in a spot of dry land that, several hours later, would be consumed by an incoming tide. In retrospect, I can't be angry because he was only trying to keep me safe.

We unloaded my gear, and he started the engine. Before I could get my bearings, a huge wave of nausea flooded over me. The choppy plane ride and lack of sleep set my stomach churning. As the pilot roared off, giving me an OK sign, I flashed back a thumbs up. Then I promptly turned, fell to my knees, and vomited into the grass. What a way to start my second journey.

Finally I was alone, but sick and suddenly nervous. At that point in my wilderness adventures, my camping skills were worse than the average Cub Scout's. The season before there had been other people around to help me out, but this time I had to be totally self-sufficient. I didn't know much about the local tides, and spent the next three hours being chased by the increasing waters. As it turned out, the tide fluctuated as much as twenty-five feet in six hours. It was not only the summer solstice, but a full moon as well, a combination that did wild things to the tides.

I finally slogged all of my gear to a suitable dry spot around three A.M. I was exhausted and still nauseated, and almost started to cry when I tried to erect the tent. I suddenly realized that I had never even tried to set up the stupid thing before now. What an idiot! I was about to collapse when I finally wriggled into my sleeping bag, and then into the flattened tent. If I couldn't get the tent up, I could at least wrap it around me and my sleeping bag and keep dry. But then I discovered another problem. The sleeping bag I had purchased, and never tried out, was built for either a small child or a dwarf. It only covered me up to my chest, leaving the rest of me cold and exposed. Suddenly, some sort of foxlike creature dashed by, yipping and screeching at my predicament. Hiding under the limp tent, I was scared and humiliated. Even on the longest day of the year, the light had all but disappeared and I lay awake, quaking in the dark, afraid of the big wild, a tough street fighter reduced to a big crybaby. My self-esteem was in a serious state of disrepair. Finally, exhaustion took over, and my dreams took me on a very strange ride.

I dreamed of large grizzlies all around me, staring and sniffing at my body. They paraded about, paw steps echoing in the inner depths of my soul. It was surreal, but for some reason not at all scary. Somehow, my sleeping brain could tell that they meant no harm.

I awoke suddenly to a sunny, beautiful day. With the dreams of the swirling grizzlies still imprinted in my memory, I looked around. There were curious divots in the ground, ground that had been smooth and featureless when I went to bed. As I propped myself up on one arm to get a better look, a shot of adrenaline rippled through my body. Struggling to free myself from the collapsed tent, I was incredulous, and pretty spooked. In the sand around my head were very fresh tracks of very large bears. The dream was real, bears were everywhere. There was no safe side of the river.

The large bear tracks got my attention, blowing my wilderness paranoia sky high. What was happening to me? I had faced many dangerous and life-threatening situations in the past, but these grizzly encounters frightened me like nothing before. I had been terrified the year before when the grizzly stood over me on the trail. Now I was even more frightened. Standing in one spot, I slowly looked around—really looked around. Then it hit me like a hammer. I was completely alone out here. There weren't any fishermen, campers, or quaint lodges with cheerful innkeepers and cable TV. As far as the eye could see, it was total wilderness. Solo as far as humans were concerned, that is, for there was an abundance of half-ton beasts with swords for claws roaming the landscape. All of them were capable of ending my life in an instant. For the first time ever, I felt small, intimidated, and vulnerable. In my moment of introspection, I had a revelation. Out here, I felt no anger. Back in the city I was always on edge, ready to lock horns with anyone who looked at me wrong. Add liquor to that equation, and I was rabid. In the big wild, I was stripped down to just me. If I were going to survive out here, I would have to pull myself together.

Determined to succeed, I untangled the maze of ropes, stakes, and wires, and set up the tent. With that accomplished, food and any other items that smelled, like toothpaste, were secured up in a tree, away from wild creatures. Grizzlies weren't the only possible bandits. Wolverines also flourished in this part of Alaska. As the largest, and possibly smartest member of the weasel family, a wolverine could destroy everything I had. After setting up a neat and functional camp, I ate heartily and slept, trying to recharge my energy.

The following day I felt fantastic. Looking out across the raging river, I could see a few scattered bears feeding on sedge grass. Aside from the bear tracks left near my sleeping spot the first evening, there were no signs of bears on my side of the river. Crossing the menacing river might be my only real hope of being among bears. But how would I do that? The river was wide, at least fifty yards across in the narrowest section. It was fed by a massive blue glacier that, due to the long light and warm temperatures, had been melting at a fantastic rate. I dropped my waterproof thermometer into the river, which was a threatening thirty-nine degrees. Suddenly, I didn't feel so fantastic anymore. What was the sense of being here if I was separated from the main population of bears by an impenetrable barrier? Crossing the river would be dangerous. Even if I crossed it, what about the grand gathering of grizzlies on the other side? How would they treat a human intruder?

The wonderful feeling I had awakened with turned sour. I packed some food, water, and my camera into a waterproof bag that fit into my backpack, and sat on the edge of the river. Crossing the river might kill me, but could I live with myself if I didn't at least try?

As I sat and debated, the thick brush behind me began to crackle and swish with the unmistakable sound of a large animal approaching. Startled, I jumped to attention, my eyes darting and straining to see the visitor. Thirty feet up the river, a golden-brown ball of fluff sprang from the brush and began moseying in my direction. From my extensive research on bears, I could tell that this animal wasn't very big or very old. It was perhaps three hundred pounds, about the size of a carousel pony, and only about two years old. It was the most beautiful bear I'd ever seen, alive or in photographs. The bear was a vision, a perfect creation that appeared to have materialized from an artist's canvas. The shiny, golden, shaggy coat was flecked with blonder tips that glittered in the warm light. The eyes were well spaced on a face that was broader than that of most brown grizzly bears. The triangular ears stood up pertly, and were tufted with fur, like that of a lynx. Within twenty feet of me, the animal stopped and sat down, peering toward me. I was ecstatic! I wasn't afraid, only worried that my presence might spook the bear. I was melting with love for the perfect animal.

"Good day, beautiful bear! Please don't be afraid. I would never harm you. You look like an angel," I said, overcome with emotion. "I love you!"

As I poured out my heart, the bear relaxed, and seemed to be enjoying the moment. Rambling on, I temporarily forgot about crossing the river. Suddenly, a name for the bear came to me. "You're just a little 'Booble,' aren't you?" I said to the golden bear. "I love you, Booble."

After several heavenly minutes, Booble stood up and strolled a few paces upriver. Then, without hesitation, the lovely creature gracefully descended into the current. It began dog-paddling with powerful, smooth strokes, a look of determination on its face. As the animal glided by, it caught my eye. In a flash, I realized that I was going to have to swim across. Nervously, I walked up to the exact spot where the beautiful animal had plunged in, and without a second thought I followed it.

The water was so cold that it shocked the breath out of my lungs. My arms and legs burned, then went numb, as if they'd been shot with Novacain. The ice-cold water was taking the fight out of me, and for a moment I thought I might drown. Just as I was about to give up, I remembered Booble's determined face as the bear had surged by me and embraced the river. "I am Grizzly, I am Grizzly," I thought, and the power returned to my limbs. I paddled just like Booble, forcing my way across. With a last burst of strength, I pulled myself up onto the bank.

Booble had arrived ahead of me and was busy wringing itself dry. A series of convulsive shakes sent water droplets flying around like a slow-motion sprinkler system. As I climbed out of the cold water, I tried to imitate Booble's shake-and-dry routine, but had less than spectacular results when I waggled my butt. Yet, thanks to the bear, crossing the river was a moment of triumph.

I followed Booble at a respectful distance, trying not to intimidate the bear. I hoped that by being polite, I might learn more from this animal. Booble hopped onto a path carved deeply through the high grass, and purposefully moved on. Nervous excitement pulsed through my veins. This was exactly the kind of adventure I had hoped for.

Without warning, a mother bear with two plump yearlings reared up out of the grass. This was the first time I'd ever seen a mother with cubs. From all that I'd read and heard, this was the most dangerous of all bear encounters. The mother stood tall, huffing in anger. She was easily over seven feet tall, and she was popping her jaws in a fearsome distress signal. The yearlings rushed to her side, gawking anxiously. I stood, frozen, barely managing to hold back a rush of urine. Poor Booble did not fare as well, and squirted like a fire hose. Because the stream of urine shot backward, I knew that Booble was a female bear. Meanwhile, the yearlings trotted over to us for a better look, intimidating Booble, who backed toward me. In response, I dropped low to the ground so that the bears wouldn't view me as a threat. The mother increased her huffs and jaw pops, trying to rein the cubs back in. Through the grass I could see Booble's head moving from side to side, glancing from me to the much larger mother bear. "Easy, Booble," I said softly, fighting to speak through my fear. "Just be still, and maybe they'll move on." Just as Booble seemed to be regaining her composure, the mother and her young continued on their way. The danger had passed. Booble continued along the path, her adopted human companion in tow.

Booble plodded along for another mile, then made an abrupt turn toward the ocean bay. As we veered off in a new direction, I saw nine bears grazing in an adjacent field. Not even in my wildest imagination did I ever think I would be among such a gathering of grizzlies. Deliberately, Booble continued forward. I followed behind, vacillating between enthusiastic excitement and fearful apprehension. Wherever she was going, I was certain that it was a place few humans had ever been.

The pathways used for centuries by grizzly bears were a minor marvel of animal engineering. For the most part, they seemed to follow the shortest distance between two points. Occasionally, the path skirted some type of hazard, like a marshy swamp. In many spots, the constant impact of heavy paw prints had left fairly deep holes in the ground. How long had they been there? Probably before the first Eskimos appeared, several thousand years ago. For me, it was simply magical to be walking along the ancient bear trails.

Booble stopped abruptly at a high crease where the grasslands kissed the beach. I was behind her, and couldn't actually see the ocean from my position because it was blocked by a slope. I could hear the unmistakable crash of waves, and the cawing of seagulls. I smelled the thick, moist, salty air of the great Pacific. From her superior vantage point, Booble scanned the panorama intensely, moving her head from side to side. I was anxious to see what she saw, but waited patiently behind her. Booble had been heading for the beach from the very start. Whatever she was searching for was out in the ocean. In a flash, Booble rumbled to the sea. I rushed up to the bank and eagerly looked around.

It was an amazing sight. The ocean had receded dramatically, due to a radical low tide. For miles along the coast, an alien terrain of sea bottom was exposed, rippling and naked. In some areas, the tide flats appeared to be as much as a mile wide. However, the greatest shock came when I noticed what lurked on the flats. A dozen or more beautiful brown grizzly bears rummaged around in the sand. What could they be searching for? I followed Booble, hoping that she would provide the answers.

Out on the flats, Booble immediately began sniffing and swiftly digging in the sand with her mighty clawed paws. With remarkable skill and dexterity, she extracted what looked like a rock, and pawed at it with her claws. The hard round clam split in two, and Booble slurped down the insides. Booble's journey had led her to the ocean for food, and had opened up a whole new world of bear behavior for me.

Once again, I decided not to crowd my new bear friend. I walked onto the vast tide flat, away from her. Wavy ridges of fine brown sand snaked endlessly, looking like pop art. Bears fidgeted and poked about in the sand. Aside from Booble, most were about a quarter mile away. I felt as if my presence didn't bother them, since a delightful air of serenity pervaded the beach. I decided to behave like the bears, and dropped to all fours. I was transforming, going through a metamorphosis. I felt wild and free.

Booble was extremely proficient at digging clams. With each extraction, I spiritedly cheered her on. As Booble and I rollicked about on the vacant ocean floor, other bears slowly meandered in our direction. I couldn't be sure if it were a coincidence, or if they were attracted by Booble's success. In a sloppy, spread-out formation, they steadily dug and sniffed their way toward us. In all, five bears were heading over.

One was a giant male of perhaps half a ton, with a regal face and a thick brown coat. Right away, this bear reminded me of a human friend I have, so I named him Warren. Another was medium in size, with frosted fur and a doglike snout. There were also two subadult bears. Research had told me that bears are subadults from the time they are two until they reach sexual maturity. Females reach sexual maturity at about five, and males at around six and a half. However, it's not unusual for male bears to be as much as nine years old before they reach sexual maturity. One subadult was light, the other dark, and both sported fuzzy punk-rock coats. But the fifth bear was the most unusual. He looked as though he'd come all the way from Russia, and if I hadn't known better, I'd have sworn he was a polar bear. He wasn't as large as the giant brown male, but with his nearly white coat he was a magnificent creature.

As the bears continued to approach, Booble became distressed. She yawned several times, a key sign of stress in bears. For a moment, I thought that she was going to flee and abandon her clam-digging endeavors. Booble sat on her bottom, looking at the wave of incoming bears, periodically glancing back at me. After several minutes of what appeared to be serious contemplation, she righted herself and tentatively stepped around me. Booble strategically stationed herself so that I shielded her from the other bears. Many times, subadult bears group together for protection, almost like young human gangs. Being a newcomer among grizzlies, her choice had me worried.

Eventually, the other bears moved and surrounded us. My head told me to remain calm and relaxed. My body didn't want to obey, and pulsed with fight or flight chemical stimuli. All of the bears bobbed, scooped, and looked toward me. None of them seemed afraid, or exhibited any aggressive signals. Instantly, I realized that my survival depended on the ability to relax in this stressful situation. Politely, I began to sing songs of love and praise to the bears. They looked at me quizzically at first, then, without concern, stopped their advances and resumed digging. Booble's nervous tension seemed to lift as well. She sniffed, scooped, and snatched clams with renewed gusto. I was overjoyed. In that moment, I truly felt at one with the grizzlies.

4

Nearly two hours later, the tide had, literally, turned. A new cycle of water, unrolling like a liquid tarp, edged its way toward all of us. The bears could not dig their clam-mining shafts underwater, and were pushed steadily back to shore. Booble and the beautiful white bear worked as long as possible. Warren, the two fuzzy subadults, and the bear with the doglike snout abandoned their digging chores and headed to the green pastures. Oddly enough, I noticed that during the morning round of digging, the others had dug close to the white bear. I decided to name him Beacon, like a shining white light. Booble and Beacon worked hard, digging like buddies in the disappearing sandy tide flat. Booble seemed safe with Beacon, so I let her be and set off for the great green fields on shore. I was aware that if I separated from Booble at this point, I might never see her again. The thought of losing touch with Booble saddened me. However, even if that wonderful morning was all I had, I'd never forget her.

As I reached the fields, the ache in my heart was quickly replaced by renewed excitement. The sprawling green fields were littered with bears. One patch boasted between forty and fifty bears. They were all sizes, shades, and ages. Most grazed, while others slept, wrestled, or mated. I slowly made my way onto the green, staying a comfortable hundred yards away for relatively safe viewing. Slinking about, I discovered a large crater surrounded by fresh piles of bear droppings, almost like sundial markings. The scat didn't smell foul, but was actually rather aromatic, like freshly cut grass. I recognized the crater from my research as being a bear daybed. Located near food sources, and often with a commanding view of the surroundings, daybeds are used by all bears for short- or long-period resting. A bear may have several daybeds within the area it lives in.[1] This bed was eight feet long, six feet wide, and three feet deep. I plopped down in the crater, and peeked out over the edge at the bears. I couldn't believe it! If anyone had ever told me that one day I'd be lying in a real grizzly bear bed with fifty of them surrounding me, I'd have thought they were crazy.

The grazing bears harvested grass with steady yo-yo chomps, then lifted their heads to swallow. Except for a few sparring subadults on the distant fringe of the field, the grazing bears were very calm. None of the bears I'd seen so far resembled the frothing, savage beasts that most people imagine. Left alone in their natural environment, they were quite peaceful. In one of nature's secret classrooms, I was learning the true ways of bears. Right then and there I vowed to continue learning as much as possible about them, and try to teach the world. Feeling a sense of contentment, my eyelids grew heavy, and I fell asleep in the bear's bed.

Slipping into a trance, bears swirled about in my head, just like in the dream I'd had the evening I arrived. Crunch! Crunch! Crunch! could be heard as if in another room of my dreams. The persistent crunching was soft and surreal at first, then louder and more realistic. Finally, I shook myself awake and found myself staring up at a huge grizzly just a few feet from my head. The animal was so gigantic that it blocked out the sun's light, its massive head larger than two basketballs put together. The bear was a deep chocolate brown, almost black. Platter-sized paws with daggerlike claws were inches from my dirt-smeared face. What was I thinking, falling asleep in some giant bear's bed? He continued to graze, glaring at me all the while. He was so close, I could have reached out and patted his damp mouth and chin. I could hear the grass slide down his gullet, gurgling around in his swollen belly. His stomach was so huge that it nearly dragged on the ground. I was terrified, yet I couldn't help but marvel at the magnificent animal. At that moment, my future rested in his paws. Without staring directly at him I sensed something unique about this bear. I began to sing, ever so softly, "Mr. Chocolate Bear, I'm sorry I'm in your way."

He cocked his head and gingerly backed up a few paces, peering at me. His jaw hung open slightly, in comical fashion. Without knowing why, I felt positive that I could roll out of the crater and safely leave. Carefully, I did just that, and crawled away from the hole, all the while singing sweetly to the bear. Once I was out, he moved forward and lowered himself into the bed. He investigated my odor, inhaling deeply where my body had been. He didn't seem angry or put out, and settled in, sprawling out flat on his rotund tummy. "Thank you, Mr. Chocolate Bear. Thank you, sir," I said, and quietly stole away.

The rush of the face-to-face encounter lifted me into a euphoric state. I practically flew back to my campsite, dancing a jig and throwing my arms into the air. When I arrived at the raging river, another transformation occurred. I no longer feared the rapids. The river still warranted my caution and respect, but not my cowardice. Summoning the power of the grizzly within me, I dove in and vigorously paddled across, snarling and growling the whole way. I was wild and free.

In the days that followed, I developed a routine for visiting the bears. The morning began with a hearty breakfast of peanut butter sandwiches, dried fruits and vegetables, and some stretching calisthenics. From there, I forged the dangerous river with a determined swim, and rendezvoused with the clamming bears. I finished off the day with a deeper exploration of the inland areas. I decided to dub the entire area the "Grizzly Sanctuary." My devotion to its inhabitants grew with each passing day.

After several visits to the clam flats, it became apparent that virtually all of the same bears were there each day. Each morning I set up in a neutral position, far enough away from the activities so as not to intimidate the bears. There were as many as twenty different individuals staggered about the flats. Occasionally the bears clumped in small groups, though none was actually working together. There didn't seem to be any thievery or conflict within the groups. Each was concerned with securing as many clams as possible during the extreme low tide.

The levels of skill and digging styles were varied, differing from bear to bear. It was fascinating—and entertaining—to study the various techniques employed by each animal. My initial guess was that the giant males would be the most proficient clammers, followed by the adult females, with subadults bringing up the rear. I thought that the large males' need for additional calories to maintain their greater body size and the fact that they could dominate the prime locations made it a cinch for them to achieve optimum success. I could not have been more wrong. Besides big Warren, two other half-ton giants, Hulk and Hefty, joined in the clamming activities. Each was ten feet in length, nose to rump, and close to five feet high at the shoulder. As expected, the dominant males bullied their way around the flats, commanding first crack at the preferred locations. Even with that going for them, their clam-digging abilities were, at best, shoddy. Warren usually lay on his big belly, digging with a decidedly halfhearted effort. Hulk and Hefty didn't fare much better, lumbering from spot to spot without much in the way of results.

Booble and Beacon had the most stylish moves, and also secured the most clams. They utilized all of their senses to achieve success. First, they located their quarry by either seeing a squirt of water emitted by the clam or by hearing it spurt from the sand. Then, with paws pointed, they zeroed in on the spot. With their sense of touch they began scooping rapidly, all the while sniffing into the developing shaft to detect the clams. As the sand piled up, they rested the left sides of their faces on extended left limbs, using them like pillows, with their fannies jacked high in the air, swaying to the beat of their labors. Finally, sometimes a meter deep, a clam would be secured, extracted, and eaten, thus gratifying their final sense—taste.

The two clamming subadults I had met previously on the flats were also excellent at extracting clams. I named the female Holly and the male Mickey. Another fluffy, chocolate-brown subadult joined in, and I named him Windy. As the subadults dug intently, their output easily doubled that of giants Warren, Hulk, and Hefty.

Then there was the final touch that separated the great clammer from the poor one. The successful bears were deftly splitting the clam shells apart with their claws in order to reach the succulent meat. But big lugs Warren, Hulk, and Hefty were too impatient for such techniques. Instead, they crushed the bivalves. This hasty shortcut left hard bits of shell that lodged in their throats as they swallowed the clams. They hacked and coughed, wasting valuable digging time.

One late morning, Warren the grizzly ran into an unusual problem that created havoc on the normally tranquil tide flats. While digging nonchalantly, a large Alaskan Dungeness crab clamped onto Warren's tender nose. Warren roared, leapt to his feet, and spun around like a cartoon character. The crab shot from his snout and landed a dozen yards away. Warren was extremely angry, and vented his pain by violently pounding the sand around him. All four subadults, Booble, Windy, Mickey, and Holly, became frightened and ran behind me for cover. Nearly crapping myself, I waved my arms and protested, "Whoa, whoa, kids! You've got the wrong idea! I'm no hero!" Beacon remained cool during Warren's violent tantrum, and continued digging mechanically. Then he sashayed past the irate Warren, picked up the discarded crustacean, and feasted on it. Soon after, Warren settled down, and order was restored to the clam flats. The subadults resumed catching dozens of clams, while the big guys loafed around.

Meanwhile, something new and wonderful had captured Beacon's attention. A beautiful adult of similar white pelage pranced about the great wide-open clam flats. Her coat shimmered and glistened in the brilliant sunlight. I named her Comet. Warren, Hulk, and Hefty abandoned their meager digging efforts and began parading toward Comet, sniffing intensely. Comet was probably in estrous, or heat, and her sexually ready condition drew the attention of the giant males. There was incredible tension on the flats as they zeroed in on Comet. However, Beacon intercepted Comet, and began playfully jogging alongside her. Beacon and Comet gently nipped and flailed at each other. Although the other giant males easily outweighed Beacon by at least two hundred pounds, for some reason they deserted their pursuit of Comet. A quarter mile away, along the heavenly beach setting of the Grizzly Sanctuary, Beacon and Comet mated. I blew them a kiss, wishing for beautiful, healthy babies.

My trip was nearing its end. On my last full day, filled with sadness, I ventured out to the clam flats one last time. As usual, Booble gravitated toward me and chose to dig close by. She seemed comfortable in my presence, and even grazed nearby in the vast inland fields of sedge grass. On our last day together, Booble was in top form, quickly securing sixty-seven clams in just over two hours. Between her grass and clam consumption, the little golden bear was blowing up into a pudgy ball. "Booble," I said, "if you keep chowing down like this, I'm going to have to pull you around on a giant wagon."

My stay in the Grizzly Sanctuary had led me to some serious introspection. As I watched Booble work, my heart ached. I felt sadness, hope, and the desire for redemption. Most of all, I truly wanted to help all bears. Yet, deep down, I knew that alcoholism owned my soul. All my promises, pledges, or covenants were worthless. Yes, out in the wild I was clean and sober. But once back in civilization, I knew that alcoholism would overcome me. No person, program, or support group could ever help. As Booble mined the sea floor, I begged her for help.

"Booble," I pleaded, tears rolling down my cheeks, "I'll never really be your defender because I can't stop drinking. I'm such a loser."

The beautiful animal edged closer, radiating happiness and contentment. She leaned into the sand, shoveling with abandon next to me. Soon, her entire right limb was buried inside her latest clam hole. I could hear the air move in and out of her lungs. In that moment, we could not have been more vulnerable. Booble trusted me with her life and I trusted her with mine. I begged forgiveness from a higher power, then made my pledge: "I will stop drinking for you and all bears, I will stop and devote my life to you."

Booble watched me calmly, then did something extraordinary. With a playful swat, she flipped a clam shell over to me. Elated by the action, I picked up the shells and stuffed these treasures into my pocket.

Many years ago, when I saved a bucket of frogs on the banks of a pond, an eco-warrior was born. Now, on a faraway beach, my battle for preservation truly began.

Back in the metropolis of Southern California, my pledge to Booble prompted an awakening. My life was no longer a monotonous blur of aimless drinking. At last I had dreams, goals, hopes, and a reason to live. Sickness, the shakes, and anxiety evaporated, and my boiling anger dissolved as well. It was like being reborn. I was determined to take the life that Booble had saved and devote it to bears, to animals of every stripe, and to ecological preservation.

During my time away from the bears, I devoured information about the species. I was shocked to learn the tragic history of the relationship between brown grizzlies and people. However, I was also filled with hope for a brighter future. In my investigations, I realized that what's good for grizzlies is also good for people.

Brown grizzlies are at the pinnacle of the ecological pyramid formed by the flora and fauna of their homes. Their existence within any given habitat is proof that the ecosystem is healthy. Therefore, preserving the habitat of bears almost certainly preserves every living thing, from top to bottom. There are important reasons for man to preserve grizzly bear habitats, for within areas where bears live, many resources exist that are directly linked to our own survival. The Tongass National Forest in southeast Alaska not only supports many bears, but is also North America's largest temperate rain forest, processing an enormous amount of carbon dioxide into oxygen. Trees are the lungs of the earth, so conserving the integrity of this habitat for bears rewards all humans with life-supporting air. In other brown grizzly wilderness areas, streams, creeks, and rivers spawn millions of salmon. Throughout Siberia, Alaska, and Canada, the fishing industry depends on pristine wilderness areas to spawn fish. In order to ensure the quality of bear habitats, these areas must remain vast, undeveloped, roadless wildernesses, free of oil spills and other human contaminants. Preserving the quality of these habitats so that they can support brown grizzlies guarantees the success of the ecosystem. For the wilderness, bears are the equivalent of the canary in a coal mine.

In America some 100,000 grizzlies once thrived in the lands

west of the Mississippi River. The 1804 Lewis and Clark Expedition was the beginning of the end for grizzlies, wolves, and wilderness habitat in the lower forty-eight states of America. The wave of settlers following the Lewis and Clark Expedition viewed the grizzly as both a threat and vermin that needed to be eradicated. Within 100 years they had nearly wiped out all of the grizzlies through a campaign of bullets, traps, and poisons. As of 1995, less than 1,000 of the original 100,000 animals remain, clinging to under 2 percent of their original habitat.

Today, the war against the grizzly rages on wherever the animals remain. The first and greatest threat is the destruction of their habitat for mining, logging, oil and gas development, or simply to build cities. Without their habitat, the bears of the world will perish. The second threat is legal brown grizzly sport hunting. Every year in Alaska, some 1,200 brown grizzlies are legally killed for trophy; hundreds more are killed in Canada, and in Russia an unknown number are sport-hunted every year. As well as legal sport hunting, illegal poaching of grizzly bears also occurs in these areas. The third threat to the survival of bears is the international trade in bear gallbladders and other body parts. Bear gallbladders have been used for over 2,000 years in traditional methods of healing throughout Asia. The gallbladder produces bile, which contains ursodeoxycholic acid, or UDCA. It has been falsely reported that UDCA is an aphrodisiac, but it is used to treat an incredible array of physical ailments, from sprains to cancer. However, natural and semisynthetic substitutes for UDCA exist, including the herb Madagascar periwinkle, rhubarb, and a derivative of cow bile. All of these are actually more powerful than any bona fide bear gallbladder. If the world's consumers of bear gallbladders would substitute these other remedies, countless bears would be saved.

Unfortunately, tradition and superstition keep up the demand for bear gallbladders. Many Westerners believe that there are fantastic profits to be made, although gallbladders extracted illegally from American bears generally sell for from between 100 to 500 dollars. Poachers would have to destroy an incredible number of bears to become wealthy. There is big money to be made, but it is from dried gallbladder, sold by the gram. In 1990, dried bear gallbladder sold in South Korea ranged from 1 dollar a gram to 210 dollars a gram. Since the average brown grizzly bear gallbladder weighs between 100 and 150 grams when dried, a large gallbladder could bring in as much as $31,500. Presently, the demand for bear gallbladders has leveled off, but there is still a huge market. Since 70 percent of all of the bear species on earth live in North America, as the bears are wiped out in Asia, the market will shift to North America, where bear gallbladders can be procured in virtually every city.

The people of Asia have been known to consume bear gallbladders as well as bear meat. South Korea is widely viewed as the bears' worst enemy. During the late 1980s and early 1990s, South Korean nationals in Thailand frequently dined on bear. It has been reported that in some restaurants bears were bludgeoned to death or were boiled alive in front of salivating patrons. When Seoul hosted the Olympic Games in 1988, thirty sun bears, an extremely endangered species, were smuggled into Korea to feed the home team's athletes.[2]

After my first season at the Grizzly Sanctuary, I knew that if people understood bears and their place in nature, there would be hope for their survival. My life's work would be to educate people about bears and to help them understand that what's good for grizzlies is, indeed, also good for people. If education was the key, then the Grizzly Sanctuary was the well of information. I believed that if I spent more time in the Sanctuary, the bears might teach me their secret ways.

5

The Timothy Treadwell who returned to the Grizzly Sanctuary the next year was a new person. I was self-assured, clearheaded, unafraid, and determined to help preserve bears. I was even prepared for the possibility of my death: Unfortunately, when a bear injured or killed a person, that bear was usually killed. So that no bear would suffer, I instructed everyone involved in transporting me to the Sanctuary to secretly dispose of my body in the event of a deadly encounter. I wanted so much to live for the bears, but if they killed me, I would rest in peace in the Grizzly Sanctuary.

Going back to the Grizzly Sanctuary felt like a homecoming. After the roar of the float plane had dwindled to a whispering buzz, I stood alone, in silence, on the edge of the Grizzly Sanctuary. I was overwhelmed by the pristine beauty of this wild, forgotten land. I felt ready for anything as I walked into the heart of the grizzlies' home.

Most of the bears were gathered on an immense grassy field that I called the "Big Green." The Big Green, covered with a grasslike plant called sedge grass (*Carex langlii*), was the most enticing spot for the bears of the Grizzly Sanctuary. Sedge grass, a food source essential to the bears in the early part of the season, is a perennial that sprouts from rootstock.[3] After the ice and snow melt in the spring, the thin, pointed blades grow to be thick and luxuriant, covering the field in a rippling green sea of vegetation. The sedge grass reaches a height of three or four feet before turning brown in late July or August. It is so important to the bears because in its early stage of growth it is up to 26 percent protein (as a percentage of its dry weight). Some of the other early food sources the bears seek in the Grizzly Sanctuary include clams, washed-up sea mammal carrion, weakened moose, moose calves, roots, and tubers. All brown grizzly bears are opportunistic omnivores, and although the bears of the Grizzly Sanctuary did eat meat, the sedge grass was their first reliably abundant source of food.

Since the Big Green was full of grizzlies eating sedge grass, I was concerned about where to pitch my tent. I decided that the middle of the Big Green was just too intense and dangerous. The far border, which paralleled the ocean, was interrupted by an elevated section of land dotted with scrubby pine trees and alder thickets. Alders are shrubs or small trees of the birch family that grow in wet ground and bear small spikes. Beneath the trees were centuries-old bear trails and bear beds carved into the flora like a secret grizzly village. I thought about setting up camp there, but decided that that would be pushing it. Instead, I set up camp in a field that led to the ocean, away from the Big Green. This area was used by the clam diggers as a route to the shore, and as a temporary rest stop. Since it wasn't an area where bears tended to linger, I figured that my camp wouldn't be a nuisance. Weeds and stalks were abundant around my site, but none offered the bears the kind of nutritional value that the sedge grass did. Tucked into this smaller field adjacent to the ocean, I would be visited by a minimal amount of bear traffic.

The bears that migrated to the Big Green were of all ages and sexes. Adult males were the easiest to identify; over 800 pounds, they were generally twice as big as adult females, and had a more pronounced shoulder muscle. Equally as easy to spot were mothers accompanied by cubs. It was the adult females and large subadult males that were harder to tell apart. In these cases, the simplest method was to observe them urinating. The female's stream of urine flows backward from the hind end, whereas all males are equipped with a hard penis bone, or baculum, that projects the urine forward.

Rain fell through the night, pattering the tent with a pleasing rhythm. The rain allowed me a guilt-free pass to sleep in, and I pulled the sleeping bag's covers over my face. At dawn, a series of odd squeaks woke me up. Feeling groggy, I just wanted to ignore the noises. After all, hundreds of different bird species migrated to and nested in the Grizzly Sanctuary. That's what it had to be, I told myself, nothing worth getting wet over. I tried to go back to sleep, but another series of squeaks punctuated the early morning quiet. It was something alive, but definitely not a bird. Without putting on rain gear I crawled out of the front of the tent. I held myself up on extended arms, as if locked in a push-up. Slowly, I craned my head about, looking in all directions. Just a few feet from the tent, a round mother bear rested on her back while three pint-sized cubs suckled at her enormous chest. The mother was calm, her eyes shut, as the dark, soggy cubs kneaded and purred in bliss. I could hear the milk gurgle as they gulped it down. Too shocked to be scared, I continued to stare until the mother opened her eyes. She gaped widely at me, inhaling vigorously. It should have been the most dangerous few seconds of my life, but I felt an odd sense of serenity. I lowered myself to the ground, face flush with the wet earth as the soft rain continued to blanket the Sanctuary, and the mother rolled her head to the side, ignoring my intrusion. The cubs nursed ravenously, occasionally squawking and bouncing to a new nipple. Then, after ten minutes, the mother lurched and righted herself. The triplets fell like bowling pins, then wobbled to all fours. As the mother began to shuffle off, the cubs spotted me. Gripped by curiosity, the tykes popped up on their hind legs and gaped at me. The mother blew a series of strong huffs from deep in her throat, calling for obedience. As the cubs dutifully complied, I smiled and gave each a name. The mother became Ms. Goodbear, and the cubs Alvin, Pete, and Scruffy.

Ms. Goodbear gently coaxed her family away, toward the incline that separated my field from the Big Green. The ridge was about eight feet high, and very steep. Ms. Goodbear dug holes in the earth, which served as a ladder for her tiny spring cubs. One by one, the miniature bears ascended the homemade steps, then disappeared into the thicket.

For days after Ms. Goodbear and her family departed, the rain persisted. The relentless storm pinned me inside, reading, writing, sleeping, and playing cards. My two-man, A-Frame tent had taken so much punishment that it sprang a leak. Small pools of water collected in the corners, forcing me to start bailing. With another few days of rain, I'd be living in a chilly Jacuzzi.

On a particularly stormy day, a steady beat of throbbing thuds woke me from a tranquil nap. The little pools of water in the corners of the tent splashed in rhythm to the increasing vibrations. Still dazed with sleep, I lifted my head to decipher the noise: This was no nursing cub. Panic surged through my body. Maybe it was some sort of Alaskan seismic nightmare.

In frantic haste I slapped on a pair of shoes, tossed a raincoat over my shoulders, and crept out of the tent. I was kneeling before one of the biggest bears I'd ever seen. If Hulk and Hefty were giants, this bear eclipsed even them. His massive, muscular frame was eleven feet long from nose to rump, and five feet high at the shoulder. If ever there were a bear over 1,500 pounds, it was right there in front of me.

The monster bear stared right through me without any hint of emotion. He was regal. He was cool. He was God, or at least knew Him. He could demolish me with a single flick of his long, sharp claws, or with a crushing bite from his forty-two teeth. A chill of terror went through my entire body as he thundered closer. I tried to steady myself. It was time for me to speak to the giant and attempt to communicate my intentions.

"Well, sir," I rasped, fighting through the cotton wad that seemed to fill my mouth, "you're not going to believe this, but I'm here to save you and all of your subjects." My voice strengthened as the giant simply watched me. "Did you know that some humans kill beautiful bears like you for sick thrills? Well, that's not going to happen while I'm here, sir."

The monstrous animal gazed at me, a calm aura surrounding him. His eyes blinked in slow motion, then he turned abruptly and sauntered off to rule his kingdom. He was the monarch of the Grizzly Sanctuary, and perhaps of all the north. I named him Czar. As he left, I sighed with relief and exhilaration. Then I took the longest piss of my life.

The next day, to the delight of all living things in the Grizzly Sanctuary, sunshine and radical low tides returned to the land. Many of the same bears I had met the year before returned, like clockwork, to harvest razorback clams in the uncovered ocean. Beacon, Holly, Windy, and Warren were all on hand, mining for mollusk gold. Even Mr. Chocolate, the kind, dark giant that had spooked me out of his bed, rambled around the clam flats in search of food. His keen nose eventually located a gooey mess of dead fur seal far from shore. Sadly, Booble wasn't anywhere in sight. She wasn't on the flats, or inland, a fact that really concerned me. It was just as well she wasn't there, for on that fateful day, men came calling with murder in their hearts.

I was sitting out in the wet sand, surrounded by eight or nine busy bears, when we all picked up the sound of an approaching boat. I focused in on the craft with my binoculars. It was forty feet long and very expensive. As the cruiser anchored, I laid down on my stomach so that they wouldn't see me. A motorized skiff from the boat headed in toward the flats. In the skiff were three humans, each with a rifle slung over his shoulder.

Mr. Chocolate was the first to sense the danger. He stood on his hind legs—soaring higher than a basketball hoop—sniffed, then galloped toward the shore. His action startled most of the others, and they scattered like a flock of birds. I focused in again on the mother ship. There were no numbers or names on the boat, which wasn't a good sign. The skiff landed, and the men hopped out, scoped rifles in hand. They immediately began stalking the closest bear. I swung my lenses and gasped in horror. They were after Beacon, the beautiful white bear! I didn't know for sure if they were going to shoot, but it didn't matter; I had to act quickly. The Grizzly Sanctuary was federally protected and it was illegal to carry a gun here. The man in the center, in camouflage fatigues, bolted his rifle. I jumped up, huffing and blowing like an angry, stressed-out bear, and Holly and Windy ran for the fields. I charged toward the men screaming, "GET THE FUCK OUT OF HERE! GO ON, GET OUT!!" One of the goons responded by pointing his rifle directly at me. There were only two choices for the men— shoot me or retreat. The men on either side of the shooter grabbed at the pointed rifle and pushed it toward the ground. Then the deadly trio jogged back to their skiff. Once the three men were back aboard the main boat, it weighed anchor and departed, never to be seen again.

Returning to the Big Green, I spotted Beacon and Mr. Chocolate grazing, without a care in the world. Animals face life-and-death threats on a daily basis; unlike humans, they can recover from dramatic events rapidly. I remained upset, and required a longer period of time to readjust. I hiked back to the raging glacial river to take a dip and clear my head.

I liked returning to the river, because it was where I first met Booble. I still hadn't seen her this year, and I was starting to worry: More than 50 percent of all brown grizzlies die by the age of five. Booble was between three and four years old, and so there was a good chance that she was dead. It just didn't seem fair that the little golden bear that had inspired me to live a decent life might not have one of her own. As the icy water rejuvenated me, I decided to comb the entire Grizzly Sanctuary, looking for Booble.

I may not have found Booble, but in a secluded corner of the Big Green, I did find Czar. He was busy feasting on tons of fresh sedge grass. I approached him respectfully, and sat on a heap of old logs that had washed up during a storm. Even though I was sitting on the pile of wood, his head was still higher than mine as he stood on all fours eating. Then he returned to the sedge grass, devouring it in rhythmic chomps. Enormous piles of grassy excrement littered the immediate area. Bear scat is beneficial to the land because it can scatter and fertilize the seeds of plants that the bear has consumed, as well as create humus, which enriches the soil. And, unlike my own, Czar's sedge grass scat actually smelled quite pleasant.

The previous incident at the clam flats made it clear that at any given moment bears could face deadly threats at the hands of man. In particular, Czar would be a coveted trophy for poachers. For such a massive animal to survive, he must be both intelligent and stealthy. Czar's presence was the stuff of Native American legend, for the Indians and Eskimos believed that bears embodied wisdom and greatness. All of the animals of the Grizzly Sanctuary deferred to Czar as their superior. Sitting with him provided a moment of cheer in the middle of my gloomy search for Booble.

"You know, Czar, it's no wonder that you never venture out into the clam flats. I reckon that you realize how easy it would be for evil humans to hurt you out there. One day I hope that humans come to understand how beautiful all of the grizzlies are and let you be completely free. Until that day comes, I'll care for you and watch over you." Czar moved closer to me. "Czar, I'm so worried! I can't find little Booble," I said sadly. "It doesn't make sense! The tides are perfect for digging clams. I wish there were a way you could tell me where she is." Gradually, Czar grazed closer, perhaps closer than he should have to me. But he was in control, steadily moving toward me. This close union with the King of all Northern Animals encouraged me to work harder for the bears. I thanked big Czar for his hospitality, bid him a temporary good-bye, and left to continue my search for Booble.

In my travels I spoke to Beacon, who was trying to nap, Mr. Chocolate, who was grazing, and Windy, who was digging roots. I saw Warren, who was busy trying to mate with a new female, and observed a bunch of new bears busy doing grizzly things. Along the way I spotted Beacon's former mate Comet shepherding a new spring cub, Saturn.

West of the Big Green, a calm creek snaked its way deep into the Sanctuary. The freshwater stream separated the Big Green from an adjacent sedge grass field. Along with the bears, numerous other animals lived by the creek. They were more secretive than the grizzlies, and harder to spot. Over time, I did manage to see river otters, a wolverine, and the occasional moose.

Continuing my search for Booble, I saw a family of red foxes cavorting about in the open. These animals were less bashful than the other species of the Sanctuary. The two parents had their paws full with the duties of raising a six-pack of glowing red pups. Mom and Dad yipped, warning the offspring to stay away from me, the strange two-legged bear. The pups obeyed and kept their distance except for one particularly ornery sibling who sneaked closer and closer to me. Each day while I patrolled for Booble, I would stop and visit the foxes. Eventually my little buddy would bolt from the cover of tall grass that bordered the creek and nip at my hiking shoes. Then he would race back to his family in a blind fury, as if fleeing for his life. Much to his parents' dismay, he became more brazen with each visit. They squealed in high yips and screeches for their wayward pup to return. On one of my visits, I learned for sure that the tyke was a male when he urinated on my tripod. "Aw, for crying out loud!" I yelled at the pup. It was just the beginning of a literal flood of urinations and poops on my possessions. The more I got to know the little bugger, the more I realized that the disobedient flaming torpedo of terror was a lot like me. One day, after he'd left the relative safety of the fox family's domain to follow me, I had no doubt what to name him. I called him Timmy the Fox.

Not long afterward, Timmy and I were patrolling the Big Green when a new male bear made his presence known. The Big Green's sedge grass was peaking in protein content, attracting a glut of giant harvesting grizzlies, including Mr. Chocolate, Hulk, Hefty, Warren, and Czar. All of the males were over half a ton in weight, with Czar the king and ruler. Garth, the new male, pushed his way around the sedge grass field, upsetting the status quo. He was second in size only to the great Czar, and by any standard was a classic grizzly beauty. Garth had silver-tipped hair on a lush, woolly coat of auburn-brown fur. His coat was shiny and well groomed, but interrupted by scars. The wounds were rather fresh, which probably meant that Garth was a fighter. Normally, Timmy and I could cruise right into the field and join the congregation of bears. Not today. We could feel the tension among the bears as Garth continued to bully his way about the sedge. One by one, Garth moved into each bear's personal space, displacing the bear from its chosen spot. Only Czar and Mr. Chocolate were immune from him. Timmy and I hung out on a distant fringe, observing the action.

We were about to leave when a small bear ambled into the field. This was not good. All day long, the smaller bears had kept their distance, nibbling on the less ample sedge grass at the edges while they waited patiently for a change in the situation. Now, this crazy little bear was about to seriously upset the tentative balance on the field.

The instant Garth spotted the intruder, he tore after it, causing most of the other bears to scatter in all directions. The little bear that started it all bolted for its life—right toward Timmy and me!

"Abandon ship, Timmy!" I cried. "Every animal for himself!"

As I turned to seek refuge, I caught a glimpse of the fleeing bear. It was Booble! Instead of retreating, I stepped out into the field and called to her, "Come on, girl! It's OK, you're home now!" As Booble galloped toward me, Garth broke off his charge and, in agitation, began biting at the grass. Booble's beautiful golden-brown fur stood straight out, as if plugged into high voltage. Her eyes gleamed in terror, and she peed herself in fright. "Calm down, girl. I got you! Everything's going to be all right," I repeated to Booble. She calmed down after a moment, and began munching on a decent patch of sedge grass. Within minutes, all of the bears in the Big Green returned to being calm. Not me! As much as I tried to be like a grizzly, I was shaking like Jell-O. Timmy the Fox emerged from a clump of small bushes. His wide eyes and damp bottom told me that he wasn't such a tough guy either.

I sat next to Booble while she grazed. It seemed much longer than a year since I'd last seen her. She was about a hundred pounds heavier, her fur blonder and more luxuriant. I was so happy to see her alive and well. After the loss of Terry Tabor, it would have been hard to face the Grizzly Sanctuary without Booble. I looked at my friend with love. "Soon, Booble, the tides will be right again for harvesting clams, and you'll have a lot of work to do," I said to the bear. "Don't you worry, I'll be right there to watch over you."

Meanwhile, I had lost track of Timmy. Looking around, I spied Ms. Goodbear with her three cubs, Alvin, Pete, and Scruffy. They were all resting out in the tall grass. On closer inspection, I noticed something odd in the mass of brown and gold fur. In the pile of dozing cubs was a strange little orange blob. I squinted in disbelief. Passed out in the middle of the babies was that darn little fox. "Psst, Timmy!" I whispered. "What are you doing, little buddy? In case you've forgotten, you're a red fox, not a grizzly bear." Timmy responded with a groggy yawn, then stretched his paw across Scruffy's back and nodded off.

Booble grazed on in peaceful innocence. "Thank goodness you're home, Booble," I said. The word "home" brought a smile to my face. For in that moment, as I looked around at Booble, Mr. Chocolate, Czar, and that little weasel Timmy nestled among Ms. Goodbear's clan, I realized that I was, at long last, home.

6

Nearly four years had passed since the day I watched Timmy the Fox sleep with Ms. Goodbear's family. Each year I had returned to the Sanctuary and lived with the bears, acquiring more information about the true ways of grizzlies on each journey. When I was away from the bears, library research and personal interviews provided me with knowledge about the animals I had lived with.

The first wave of brown bears (*Ursus arctos*) crossed into North America through a land bridge at least 40,000 years ago. The bridge is now underwater, hidden beneath the Bering Sea of Alaska. The brown grizzlies spread throughout Alaska, much of Canada, parts of the United States west of the Mississippi River, and Mexico. Among the luckiest bears were the ones that migrated to the Grizzly Sanctuary. A virtual bear paradise, the isolated area overflowed with fish, plants, shellfish, and wild game. The bears prospered, and grew to be the largest found on earth. Between 6,000 to 9,000 years ago, long after the bears arrived, the first humans appeared. They were the Yupik Eskimos. Yupik Eskimos settled near the Grizzly Sanctuary and competed with the animals for resources. The bears tolerated the Eskimos, although life and death struggles occurred occasionally. Yupik warriors who took on the great bears employed a brave technique. They would jam a spear into the ground, with the sharp point angling toward the sky. Then they would purposely enrage a bear into charging. The Eskimos hoped that when the bear rushed them, it would impale itself on the sharp spear. Unfortunately for some Eskimos, it didn't always work.

Sometimes, bears terrified the Eskimos during the frozen winter. Although bears do undergo an extended period of sleep in the winter, it isn't the absolute dormant hibernation that many other animals experience. The body temperature of a hibernating grizzly drops about only five degrees Centigrade, while its heartbeat may drop from forty to eight beats per minute.[4] The bear will not eat, drink, or urinate during its entire hibernation period, which may last for six months or longer. Metabolic water is produced from fat, and the bear does not produce products of protein metabolism, which require urinary excretion.[5] However, some bears do not hibernate at all, while others occasionally leave their dens during their period of seasonal dormancy. It was some of these wandering animals that became the Eskimo's feared "winter bear."[6] Sooner or later, the strolling bear would find a patch of open water in an otherwise frozen winter, and while refreshing himself, he would wet his fur. Then he would roll in the snow, and so acquire a thick plate of ice. This icy shield wasn't a bother to the bear, but it worked to the disadvantage of the Eskimo, whose arrows and spears broke against the armoring ice. It could even stop a bullet. The winter bear became the stuff of legends.

In 1741, Russia sent Danish explorer Vitus Bering on a voyage to Alaska that would change Alaska and the Grizzly Sanctuary forever. In the course of exploring the area the Russians realized that the wildlife had incredible value, particularly the fur-bearing sea mammals. Of all the colonial powers that have ever taken over a foreign land, perhaps none were crueler than the Russians. They enslaved the Aleut and Yupik Eskimo tribes and forced them to hunt the marine wildlife of the coastal region of Alaska for fur. In 1786, the Pribilof Islands off the coast of western Alaska had 2.5 million fur seals. Under the imperialist Russian invaders, nearly every fur-bearing sea mammal was destroyed. The waste was tragic: The Russians had to stockpile the pelts between journeys back to their land, and in 1803, 700,000 Pribilof seal fur hides had to be thrown out after rotting in storage for seven years. The Russians were not as concerned with grizzly bears because their pelts offered little in the way of monetary value. Entire native populations were killed by the Russians directly, or by the diseases they introduced to the region. Consequently, the Yupik Eskimo settlements surrounding the Grizzly Sanctuary vanished. The bears ruled alone again until the era of human air travel. In the early 1900s, the Grizzly Sanctuary was officially declared a protected zone by the United States government, making it off limits to hunting and development. Yet due to the remoteness of this vast area of wilderness, legal enforcement was nearly impossible. For much of the twentieth century, the bears, moose, and caribou of the Sanctuary have been hunted by greedy poachers who arrive via float planes and boats.

To expand my research, I personally interviewed some convicted poachers. One told me that between 1970 and 1990, he killed more than 1,000 grizzlies. His favorite hunting ground? The Grizzly Sanctuary. I recalled how I had shielded Beacon from intruders years before. It was clear that I could not only learn from the bears by living with them, but that I could also protect them from illegal poaching while I was there.

With this in mind, I returned to the small Alaskan outpost nestled along the Pacific Ocean in early June of 1995. I had launched my five previous visits into the wild from this tiny town. The air-

port was buzzing with the hustle and bustle of incoming fishermen, outgoing families, and transient tourists on their way to
expensive adventures. Hugging, handshaking, and farewells filled
the large single room that constituted the airport's entire terminal.
In the previous years, there had always been some enthusiastic person to greet me and haul my minor mountain of gear to a warm
hotel. Times had changed. This town had a long history of making
a lot of money from sport-hunting bears, and it had become clear
to many exactly what I was about. For the bear killers, I was just
another eco-faggot Yankee from the lower forty-eight trying to
take away their god-given right to shoot wildlife for fun and profit.
On my return to this Alaskan town built on its reputation for fishing and hunting, I was shunned for my passionate desire to fight
for the persecuted and very misunderstood bears. I didn't mind
being shunned, but if my grizzly preservation work became successful, it might just get dangerous for me here.

A call to the float plane operator informed me that my flight to
the Grizzly Sanctuary would leave in approximately three hours.
This was plenty of time to zip over to Trapper Pete's Sporting
Goods Store for a few serious camping supplies.

Inside the front window was a stuffed trophy grizzly bear
snarling like Charlie Manson in a maximum security jail cell.
Trapper Pete's didn't carry much that most folks would consider
traditional sporting goods, like tennis rackets or baseball bats.
Instead, there were guns and bullets for blowing away bears,
moose, caribou, deer, or any other animal unfortunate enough to
get in the sights of a satisfied customer. There were lots of other
death toys like high-velocity bows, a full line of four-season trapping snares, and, of course, fishing equipment, so that an angler
could gouge and release a multitude of fish in a day and keep only
one.

I asked the clerk, Willy, for a moderate list of goods, ranging
from tarps to batteries.

"You heading out into the wilderness for a while, aren't you? What are you planning?" he asked.

I sputtered for a couple of moments, debating whether I should speak the truth or downplay everything. Ecstatic enthusiasm won out.

"I'm heading out to live with bears for the next three months," I blurted out.

"Shee-it! You crazy son of a bitch!" Willy gasped. "This is my first week working at Trapper Pete's, but I know that what you need is right over here, my man. Let me introduce you to Mr. Winchester and his good friend, Mr. Remington," Willy said proudly, his hand on my shoulder. "You are planning to take some artillery along, aren't you?" he asked.

"No, I'm not, sir. I love them too much to ever hurt one," I replied.

"Listen here," Willy continued. "You just can't trust the bears. Get yourself some protection, or head across the street and order a casket at the mortuary. That is, if there's anything left of you to bury."

Willy graciously helped me find each of my requested items. We were from different worlds, he and I. Yet, if bears were ever to have a chance, it would be vital to win the support of people like Willy. Intrigued by my life's work, Willy quizzed me inside and out.

"How in God's name did you ever get started on this nutty stuff?" Willy asked.

"That's a story too long and strange to tell you today," I answered.

After I paid for my purchases, Willy shook my hand. "If by chance you do survive this trip, be sure to come by and tell me all about it," he said.

"You got a deal, Willy," I said. "Thank you for all of your help." With that, I stumbled out the door, past the glaring eyes of the stuffed bear. As I walked to the float plane dock, my head was already swirling from what promised to be an extraordinary journey.

A dozen or more pontoon-clad flying contraptions bobbed in the seaport of this Alaska outpost town. One was about to whisk me off to the Grizzly Sanctuary. Loading the last of my bulky provisions into one of the float planes, I realized that Expedition '95 was truly underway. At last the steel-blue Dehaviland Beaver choked, sputtered, and roared to mechanical life. The owner, a bush pilot named Bob, steered the craft across a murky pea-green channel. Bob was about forty, with a cheerful face and sandy-blond hair. He exuded an air of confidence, and I was happy to be in his care.

The plane gathered speed like an old locomotive train, then lifted into the sky toward the Grizzly Sanctuary. As the plane climbed, the small town shrank away into the distance. With it, the convenience and security of human civilization disappeared as well.

This trip promised to be the most ambitious expedition among the bears that I had ever attempted. For over ninety days, I would try to live in the presence of the great bears. To succeed, I would have to move into four different grizzly ecosystems to keep up with the migrating bears. The plan was to start in the Grizzly Sanctuary. Then I would travel on into three other different habitats that I had explored briefly in the previous two years. Although you can never take anything for granted in the wild, the Grizzly Sanctuary was pretty familiar territory to me. I was anxious to try and camp in some new areas where fishing was a bigger part of the bears' lives. I hoped that I would get to know more bears in different parts of the wilderness, and would be able to observe different fishing techniques and behavioral patterns. The three additional grizzly habitats offered many important opportunities and increased dangers. Primarily, I had learned that the bears of these areas had been harassed and had even been the victims of poachers. My visits would offer a shield of safety for the bears. The additional habitats also had large runs of salmon, enticing a greater number of bears from later in the summer through the autumn. Each of the salmon fishing locations within these areas were unique from one another. It would be fascinating to study and learn about the ways of these bears, and the potential wealth of information might help in my educational campaign back in civilization. Another possibility was that some of the bears I had studied in the Grizzly Sanctuary might even migrate to one of these habitats. That would offer me the chance to learn about particular bears over a longer period of time. Since I did not have as much knowledge about bears in these habitats, the risk of rejection was real, making my endeavor more dangerous. No modern human had ever attempted to live among the grizzlies of these wild areas, and I was determined to try. I felt that it was a challenge I could not resist, and an opportunity to delve further into the secret ways of bears. I would have to become as much like a grizzly as possible to pull it off. As in all previous expeditions into the areas I visited, I would not use fire or carry a gun or two-way radio.

Bob was concerned about the conditions along the Pacific Ocean because he needed clear visibility and calm seas to land. Since the Grizzly Sanctuary was over 100 miles from the nearest town, an accurate advance weather report for the area was never available. There weren't many float plane pilots qualified, or willing, to land along the dangerous shores of the Grizzly Sanctuary.

As we flew out along an inlet of the Pacific Ocean, the high ceiling of bland gray clouds broke up into brilliant sunshine. The ocean below appeared to be a massive, frozen sheet of turquoise stained glass.

"I've been flying this route for over a decade," Bob commented over the headset, "and that, Timothy, is about as dead calm as she gets. Looks like you're going home to your bears for sure!"

It was a relief knowing that Bob never second-guessed what I was doing. Other pilots thought that I was weird or stupid, and most were positive that I was crazy. Even though Bob believed in my grizzly preservation work, and supported it with the flights, he was still extremely concerned for my safety. A devout Christian, he and his family remembered me in their nightly prayers. I truly appreciated their thoughts.

As we soared into the air space of the Sanctuary, I spotted numerous balls of moving brown fur below. "There's a mother and cubs!" I yelled. "Over there, looks like Mr. Chocolate! Hey! Two moose! Those moose better watch it, because it looks like there are at least forty bears around!" I shouted. Then he glided in and landed gently, like a swan in a lake. The tide was heading out, so we quickly unloaded my gear. If the pontoons stuck in the sand, Bob would be marooned for at least eight hours. Although Bob was a hearty Alaskan, he had no desire to sleep among the bears.

While tossing the bags and boxes on the beach, I noticed a fluffy orange ball bouncing toward us. I zoomed in with my binoculars for a better look. "Uh-oh, Bob, you better get going," I warned, "because here comes that rascal Timmy the Fox."

"You're right," said Bob, flinging out the last pack. "He's more trouble than a box of fireworks." Bob had assisted me before, and knew all about Timmy the Fox.

Bob shook my hand and jumped aboard the plane. Cranking the engine, he leaned out of the pilot's window and shouted, "Good luck and God bless! And listen, if the bears or that loony fox give you too much trouble, don't be afraid to give up. I'll come and get you any time."

"Thank you so very much, Bob!" I said and bowed, not bothering to explain that my gear didn't include a two-way radio, or any other communication device. No matter what happened, I was there for the duration.

As Bob's plane took off, Timmy the Fox jumped about like a

live wire. I patted him and bent down to kiss his head. Another fox burst toward us and quickly joined the excitement. It was Timmy's lifelong mate, Kathleen, who I had named two years before after my longtime friend Kathleen Parker. A belly full of active teats told me that there was more family around.

"Oh, boy, Timmy, don't tell me that you're a daddy now," I exclaimed, inspecting my bags for Timmy's urinary assaults. "I'm not sure that the bears and I can handle any more 'Timmys.' God help us all." Timmy and Kathleen ricocheted around my possessions, hastily inspecting every piece. I loved that Timmy, but wondered what he'd wreck in the coming season.

I had made a major strategic decision well before the start of this expedition. I was not going to camp on the safe scrubby field as in years past, but right on the edge of the Big Green. The Big Green was ground zero, a veritable grizzly city. By living on it, I would be able to study the bears twenty-four hours a day. Providing, of course, that the bears accepted me. According to my research, no human had ever attempted to live so close to so many bears.

It was almost a kilometer from the shore where I landed to the Big Green. The three hours it took to lug my stuff to the campsite would have been arduous and boring if not for my entertaining old pal Timmy. It was surprisingly hot, at least seventy degrees in the shade, yet Timmy followed along, full of pep. At one point, he bounced up and down on the thigh-high grass as if on a trampoline. Then Timmy pounced on a vole, devoured it, and quickly caught back up with me. Our route took us from the difficult deep sand of the beach, across the overgrown field of scrub grass where I had camped in previous years, and up the reliable dirt ladder Ms. Goodbear had carved several years before. We trudged along the lush old bear paths, and finally out into the Big Green.

Even though it was still early June, the Big Green was full of brown grizzly bears. Usually, it was much later in the month before bears migrated and gathered here. This meant that the probability of bears visiting my tent increased greatly, which had me a bit worried. I wondered anxiously whether it really was a sound decision to camp on the Big Green. I decided to give it a solid try, and if it became too scary, I would withdraw to the relative safety of the scrubby field.

Finally, after five round trips, I had moved all of the gear to my chosen campsite. Exhausted, I took a small break with Timmy the Fox. After some refreshments we set up the tent, a roomy three-man Lunar Ship donated by Northface. Then, with checklist in hand, I inventoried and arranged the stock for my expedition.

In addition to the tent, I had a sleeping bag, flashlights, and hundreds of rolls of film. My camera equipment, including lenses, was provided by Minolta. Thanks to Minolta, I had up-to-date photographic equipment that I couldn't possibly have afforded on my own. This photographic equipment is vital to the success of my work.

I also had a portable AM/FM radio, a pillow, waterproof duffel bags, a water filter, water containers, tarps, a mini gas stove that I rarely used, hats, bandannas, batteries, a thermometer, binoculars, a tape recorder, a rain gauge, eyeglasses, sunglasses, towels, clothing, notepads, pens, a calendar, playing cards, reading materials, a battery-powered shaver, razors, shaving cream, toothbrush, toothpaste, body lotion, sunscreen, bug nets, aspirin, trash bags (everything went in and was flown out), bear mace, fanny packs, and food. The food consisted of peanut butter and jelly, bread, dried fruits and vegetables, cereal, candy, cookies, crackers, canned tuna fish, carrots, apples, bananas, grapes, and melons. My one vice was a case of Coke, which I rationed to one can a day, usually in the morning.

My sleeping bag had been willed to me by a dear friend, Sharon. She was a beautiful, strong, athletic California girl brimming with youthful vigor. She was an accomplished triathlete, but during the peak of her career, she was diagnosed with cancer. One year later, while I was sleeping snugly in Sharon's bag among the grizzlies, she passed on. It gets quite cold in the Grizzly Sanctuary, yet Sharon's gift keeps me safe and warm.

The long day's hard work left me exhausted but not sleepy. I decided to take a short walk around the immediate Sanctuary area, and reacquaint myself with the surroundings. Feeling energetic early into the walk, I just kept going. Soon I found myself over a mile away, approaching the Sanctuary's dividing center creek.

The center creek performed several important functions for the Grizzly Sanctuary. Besides being a supply of fresh water, it also brought the strongest run of spawning salmon later in the summer months. In the early season, it was perhaps the key reason for the incredible gathering of bears. At each high tide, the ocean water advanced to the outlet of the center creek and dammed up the flow, filling the fields with fresh water. The flats alternately dried out and flooded twice daily. Due to these conditions, dense sedge grass flourished. The Grizzly Sanctuary has an annual precipitation of over sixty inches, which is distributed fairly equally over the course of the year. The rain and the center creek naturally irrigate the sedge grass fields.

The center creek was always fairly deep, and even at low tide, it could be more than six feet deep. Across the creek was a sedge grass field that I called "the Playpen." The name might sound whimsical, but I took the Playpen very seriously because a large number of younger subadult bears lived there.

Adolescent bears, particularly males, are most likely to act aggressively toward humans. Although a human of average strength should be able to ward off an aggressive subadult bear, in the mid-eighties, a Swiss woman visiting Yellowstone National Park was killed and eaten by a young male grizzly. It is particularly important to keep bears from pushing people around because, once learned, they will continue to exhibit this behavior. For the most part, people are safer traveling in groups in grizzly habitats.

All brown grizzlies offer a variety of behaviors signaling moods, from passive to aggressive. Ears back, yawns, head shakes, the grinding of teeth, woofs, and jaw pops are all indications of a stressed or possibly angry bear. Four major forms of aggression that might result in violent contact are shown by bears: challenge threats (ears back, mouth open with jaws exposed, head level and down), bite threats (head thrown upward before lowering it again), charges, and actual attacks.[7]

I had only one rule in the event of an aggressive encounter: If it was a subadult, I returned its aggression by charging back. With adult males, adult females, and mother bears, I would have to decide which course of action to take as each encounter unfolded. The best strategy was to offer these bears as much safe personal space as possible, and therefore avoid any adverse situations.

Nervously, I thought about crossing the center creek and exploring the Playpen. However, an incident from the year before convinced me to hold off—for now.

I had been watching LuLu with her son Cupcake. When Cupcake was younger, he had been fascinated by me. Whenever he spotted me he would head over, but his mother, LuLu, always huffed him back to her side. I felt bad for Cupcake because he was a solo cub and had no one to run and play with. As we watched each other from a distance, I had wished I could get to know this curious little bear better.

Last year Cupcake was two and a half, and usually at this age bears are on their own. However, Cupcake was still hanging around his mother. So was a big male who was sniffing LuLu's back end with obvious sexual intentions. Cupcake panicked and bolted right toward me, with LuLu and the large male in pursuit, putting all three on a collision course with me. I tried to divert them by leaping up and shouting. The two older bears spotted me and immediately retreated toward the woods, but Cupcake contin-ued to charge.

Determined not to fall prey to the obstinate subadult, I had continued my bluff; Cupcake snorted, bearing down upon me full force. His jaw hung open, and there was a maniacal glint in his eye. I couldn't just stand there so I rushed him, snarling and growling. As we headed toward each other, Cupcake glanced back, looking for LuLu. When he realized that his bodyguard was nowhere in sight, Cupcake broke off his charge and sprinted away from me, anxious to find his mother.

As I had watched Cupcake disappear over the field, I had realized that he was no longer the sweet cub I had met a couple of years earlier. As a subadult, he was low man on the totem pole, but still had LuLu to back him up. Perhaps he needed someone to push around and thought I was the perfect target. Or he might have recognized me, and was simply as inquisitive as ever. Maybe he was just trying to play, but his antics could kill me. At that moment, I had realized that Cupcake was a force to be reckoned with, a bear that I could not simply observe peacefully in the Grizzly Sanctuary.

Now, sitting by the center creek, I looked around the Grizzly Sanctuary for Cupcake. He was nowhere to be seen, but I spotted eleven bears in the Big Green, seventeen in the Playpen, four in between the two fields, and another seven heading from the mountains through the boggy swamps. It was very early June, and at least thirty-eight bears had arrived. I intended to keep a safe distance from the bears early in the expedition, since migrating grizzlies tend to be wary and shy when they first enter common habitats. It's almost as if they've forgotten during the long winter's sleep how to tolerate one another. This year, we would all need time to gradually get to know each other again.

I returned to the tent four hours later from the planned fifteen-minute hike, pleased that old friends Windy, Hefty, Tar, and Mr. Chocolate were already on the Big Green. I climbed into my tent and fell asleep watching them graze.

I'd just nodded off when the tent was filled with the sound of snorts, then an audible rush of bear breath. A grizzly had stopped by, curious about the synthetic blue structure. His snout and paws pressed into the walls. The tent wouldn't last long if I didn't react quickly.

"Get out! Get out, you big dog!" I unzipped the front and poked my head out. A moderately sized, 700-pound male was sniffing around. "Out of here, mister!" I commanded, clapping my hands. "Get along!" He hesitated, then moved back about 25 feet, near a pine tree, and began to dig furiously. I immediately realized that he was not excavating my grave, but his own bed for the evening. The tree swayed considerably as he ripped heaps of earth from the ground. His exaggerated physical efforts signaled anger, which was probably directed at me. However, he promptly hunkered down and fell asleep. Fortunately, unlike humans, brown grizzlies don't hold grudges. Warily, I tried to sleep, wondering what would happen next.

The next full day was spent taking an inventory of the bears. I'd already spotted Mr. Chocolate, Windy, Hefty, and Tar. I found Warren performing the traditional June ritual of mating. He wasn't the only one participating in sexual intercourse: May, June, and early July are the peak months for sexual activity among brown grizzly bears.

Since, compared to other terrestrial mammals, grizzlies have a low reproductive rate, it was great to see so much romance on my first patrol of the Grizzly Sanctuary. Females generally become sexually mature at five. They have two distinct estrous cycles, lasting from seven to ten days during the months of May, June, or July. I've also been fortunate enough to see some mating in early August. Males become sexually mature between five and eight. However, young males usually do not participate in mating activity because the older, larger males monopolize the females. The courting male bear usually has sex with the female only once a day to maximize its sperm count. Fertilized eggs result in zygotes that divide and quickly grow into blastocysts. The blastocysts do not immediately attach themselves to the uterine wall as in other mammals. Instead, they continue to float free in the womb, held in a state of suspended animation until the mother enters the den in autumn. This miracle of delayed implantation permits the mother two specific advantages: One frees her from the nutritional demands of growing fetuses, while the other enables her body to make an assessment of how many cubs she could safely give birth to and support during winter dormancy. The number of cubs she actually bears depends on how many eggs she produces, and the amount of body fat she has to sustain them.[8] Although the total gestation period is around 235 days, the actual growth time for the fetus after delayed implantation is about 6 to 8 weeks. By the end of the day, I had observed seven mating pairs. If all went well, the Sanctuary would be filled with cubs next year.

The second evening brought more close-up bear visits. First, a cute blond subadult waddled by and took a brief sniff at the tent. It was eleven P.M., and the sun still hung brightly above the horizon. I wiggled out of the sleeping bag and out into the evening light. The little three-hundred-pound bear reacted politely, exhibiting no evident signs of aggression. "Good evening, lovely bear," I said. The subadult tipped its head slightly, blinked, then stepped daintily into the nearby trees, searching for a place to sleep. Clearly, as long as I was camped out on the Big Green, a constant stream of curious visitors would be stopping by. The area I had chosen was one of their primary sleeping grounds, which made me realize that it may have been an unrealistic goal to try to camp on the Big Green.

A few hours later another bear huffed and puffed just in front of the tent. I stuck my head out again, and was startled to see Tar, eight hundred pounds of shiny dark fur and rippling muscle. I had known Tar for years, and he had always seemed to be a low-key fellow. "Hey, boy! How are you? You're really growing into a fine-sized bear!" Tar gazed at me and blinked, then waddled off into the Big Green. Tar was the last visitor . . . that night.

The next day was beautiful. Just twenty feet from my tent, Booble sauntered by with two portly yearlings in tow. During the 1993 and 1994 visits, I had not been able to locate Booble. Once again, I was forced to believe that she had died during the long, cold winter. But now, here she was, alive and right in front of me: Booble had been hiding her newborns, waiting until they were strong enough to enter the Grizzly Sanctuary.

As the trio played in the grass nearby, I could see that Booble had a nice, balanced family—one boy, one girl. I named the girl Ginger, and the blond, fuzzier male Fresca. I'm sure that I was prejudiced, but they were the most beautiful cubs I'd ever seen. As they meandered closer, I spoke to them.

"Look at how big and healthy you are. You've come a long way since that day you taught me how to cross the river. Now look. Those yearlings of yours aren't much smaller than you were then. I'm so happy to be able to watch you and your children grow. We're family, you know. I'll always be here for you."

Mother bears raise their offspring for about two and a half years. In February, while asleep, grizzlies give birth to blind, tooth-less, and nearly naked cubs. At birth, they're only nine inches long and about a pound in weight, yet they emerge from the den in the spring weighing from ten to twenty-five pounds. Most grizzlies have two to three cubs per litter, though litters of five to seven have been reported. Newborns are called spring cubs, or cubs of the year. The following season, like Booble's young, they are called yearlings. If they survive that year, they generally den with the mother again. Once the cubs are two and a half, the mother usu-ally goes back into estrous, mates again, and leaves her cubs to fend for themselves.

Returning with my camera, I watched as Ginger chomped on

sedge grass, copying, bite for bite, her mother's routine. Fresca, a typical boy, was more interested in other activities such as rolling over and playing with his toes, or stalking and chasing insects. He was especially interested in me, stretching and straining to catch a look, occasionally wandering close. I cautioned him to stay near his mom, but he ignored me. Booble usually reined him back in with a series of soft, firm huffs.

Booble and the kids hung around for two hours, delighting me with their antics. Just when I was beginning to believe they were settling in for the long haul, a male named Monster spoiled the party. He thundered by and Booble and crew hightailed it to a quieter pasture. I didn't see them again for two days, which worried me given the high mortality rate for cubs.

Approximately 35 percent of all cubs do not survive their first year. About 60 percent do not make it to the typical separation age of two and a half. There are myriad ways in which cubs can have their lives cut short: Starvation, falls, drowning, and disease are common. We humans, as always, have added threats that can contribute to cub death: electrocution, trains, cars, poaching, traps intended for other animals, cruel hunters, scared hunters, and habitat destruction. Sadly, cubs are occasionally killed by other bears. The causes of bear infanticide aren't known, but this phenomenon is probably why mother bears are so vigilant; it's well known that mother bears with cubs are extremely dangerous.

Yet I have found in the Grizzly Sanctuary that the mothers are among the safest bears for me to be around. In most cases, I have known these mothers since they were younger, were even cubs themselves, and my presence in the Grizzly Sanctuary has never been a threat to them. However, I knew that mothers with cubs could still be incredibly dangerous, and I never approached family groups, always letting them dictate the distance.

In the days that followed, sexual activity was rampant in the Grizzly Sanctuary. Everything was going really well for Tar. Now eight, he was moving into his best years. At his side was a golden-brown female in estrous I named Daisy. For the first few days of Daisy's heat cycle, the two were inseparable. If I'd ever seen bears head over heels in love, it was Daisy and Tar. They had passionate sex once a day and spent the rest of the time doting on each other. Then one hot afternoon, giant Hulk strutted in and separated the pair. Hulk eclipsed Tar by a couple of hundred pounds and a few feet in length. It was clear that in the bear hierarchy Tar was no match for Hulk. Nature can be cruel, and Tar had no choice but to retreat from his beloved Daisy. Yet Daisy still managed to sneak away from Hulk and attempted to run off with Tar. Hulk tracked Daisy down and claimed her by having sex on the spot. Tar plodded away sadly. He trudged along the stream, and sat down near me. "Tar," I said, choosing my words carefully, "that's the story of my life. If I had a dollar for every time I got dumped, we'd be millionaires." We sat by the creek chewing on grass while I shared tales of past broken hearts.

Not all of the bears were preoccupied with sex, but they all had the need for food. For the bears in the Sanctuary, the seafood of choice is razorback clams. I am not quite sure how the bears know it is a low tide, because the Pacific Ocean cannot be seen from the sedge grass fields. Yet as soon as a radical low tide occurs, the bears appear. Can they hear the change in the water's action? Or smell the exposed beach sand from far away? Perhaps there is something built into their physiology that we humans don't possess. I hope to find out one day. Until then I'll use a tide chart and meet the experts on the flats.

During the first day of low tides the flats were covered by a thick, blowing fog. The visibility was only about twenty feet. I knew that the fog concealed several huge animals with lethal claws, yet I crept out onto the flats. I could hear the scrapes and snorts of the clamming bears. The first bear I came upon in the fog was Nestlé, a chocolate-colored male who was on his way to work. The sudden encounter surprised us both. Nestlé communicated his stress with a mild yawn from unhinged jaws, and a hint of raised fur between his shoulder blades. The first priority of my work was to respect the wishes of all of the animals in their wilderness home, so I backed off and disappeared into the swirling fog.

Minutes later, I heard the huffs and shuffling paws of several bears. Suddenly, Booble, Fresca, and Ginger popped out of the heavy cloud, directly in front of me. They were startled, and Fresca stood up on his back legs, gawking nervously. I had to let them know it was me, their friend Timothy, not a rival bear. With the strange weather, I couldn't be sure that Booble would tolerate my presence near her family. I sang out, "Hi, Booble! Hi, Fresca! Hi, Ginger! It's just your friend, and no one is going to hurt you." It worked, and Booble settled her cubs and began digging for clams. I backed away to give them some space, but distance didn't seem to be what Booble wanted. She moved her family toward me, shadowing my every step. The fog seemed to have her spooked, and she was once again seeking my protection. At times, the family dug within twenty to thirty feet of me. The little bears imitated their mother and dug tiny holes, heaving sand in all directions with their pint-sized paws. They were so close that I could hear their breathing. Occasionally, a bear looked amiably in my direction. I pinched myself in disbelief, elated by their trust.

Before the tide started rising, I left Booble and her family. The fog was lifting, which gave me an opportunity to investigate other bears. I wanted to get a total count of the participating animals. Nestlé, Booble, Ginger, and Fresca made four. In the past, I'd seen as many as sixteen bears clamming on the beach at one time. Heading north, I discovered five more clammers. In the distance, I saw a mother with three new spring cubs. Observing through my binoculars, I watched as the little cubs tried to keep up with their mother. With every three steps she took, the cubs took nearly a dozen frantic strides. Like these, most spring cubs are a dark brown, turning golden blond as yearlings. When mom had enough of the clams, she headed inland. The mother's path took her across a small creek, which she crossed with little effort. To the babies, it may as well have been the Mississippi River. The cubs dog-paddled across, bawling in terror. The mother waited patiently on the opposite side, huffing urgent orders to hurry up. It was then that I realized that this bear was LuLu, the lovely mother bear that raised the not so wonderful Cupcake. Even though I was curious about Cupcake, I wasn't anxious to see him after our encounter last year in the Playpen. LuLu was finally free of Cupcake, and totally occupied by her new spring cubs. I was fairly sure that all three of these new cubs wouldn't add up to the difficulty of one Cupcake.

As in most wilds, there was a distinct ebb and flow to everything in the Sanctuary. Everything seemed subject to change—the weather, the tides, and the moods of the individual bears. One moment, the sun would be shining, and the whole Sanctuary would be at peace. The next, it would be cold and raining, dampening everyone's mood. Similarly, one day I'd be in heaven, the next I'd be struggling for survival.

After my big day at the clam flats, I was exhausted and went to bed earlier than usual. A huge crashing noise outside the tent woke me. I jerked open the door and screamed. Just above my head was the chin of a massive beast. In the slow-motion seconds that followed, I actually saw the bear's saliva drip onto my hiking shoes. My scream startled the big male, and he twisted and retreated ten feet. Then he turned to face me. His body was carved with scars, and clumps and patches of fur were missing from his coat. His bottom jaw hung askew, exposing jagged yellow teeth. Instantly, I recognized him. It was Monster, perhaps the ugliest bear in the world. Now I was really awake.

I charged, stopping just short of the bear. He reacted by standing up on his hind legs, stretching to his full ten feet. With a mouth full of foam, he tossed his head wildly while I stood my ground, growling fiercely. He dropped to the ground and galloped off, stopping halfway across the field to glare at me. Monster was large, even by Grizzly Sanctuary standards. Not the size of Garth or Czar, but probably 1,000 pounds and 8 or 9 feet long. Monster was obviously a successful bear, since his round belly dragged across the ground even in June, a lean time for bears in the Sanctuary. My instincts told me that getting Monster to withdraw had saved my life. Bravado can sometimes be the best counterstrategy with bears—I certainly couldn't have waited to see if Monster would simply have gone away. Still shaking, I looked around the Big Green. Booble, Ginger, and Fresca were chomping on one side as Tar worked another. I sang them a good-night song, told them I loved them, and crawled back into the tent. Suddenly, I realized that I had forgotten something. I leaned back out of the tent and called into the night, "I love you, too, Monster!"

7

The next morning all that remained of the fog was a light mist. Booble, Ginger, and Fresca were at work on the clam flats. Ginger, like her mother, was becoming a world-class clam digger. No longer content to mimic and play, she had already advanced to a level beyond most adult bears, resting her forehead on her left outstretched paw while digging with the right. Once she had secured a clam, Ginger balanced it with the tip of her nose against the sand and gently pried the shells apart.

Unlike his mother and sister, Fresca was not an expert in the flats. He spent his time watching his sister, intrigued by her actions but making no attempt to copy them. At times, he stood behind Ginger and got a snout full of flying sand. When he did try, he'd usually lose his balance and tumble on his butt. Clamming was important, but fortunately Fresca's survival did not rest on that single skill. He was as plump as his sister, so it was obvious that he was better suited for munching sedge grass—an activity that required no skill at all.

Booble began to let the cubs move closer to me than they were to her, a behavior that testified to the special bond I shared with this beautiful animal. When the young male Nestlé gravitated toward the activity, Booble cleverly positioned me between him and her family. Nestlé approved the arrangement by digging without concern.

Later in the clam session, Timmy the Fox joined the party, nibbling at unfinished bits that the bears had left behind, and even digging his own clam holes. I had often seen foxes and birds of prey scavenging for the uneaten clam meat that bears had left. However, Timmy was the first and only fox I ever saw digging his own clams. Unfortunately, procuring the clam was only half the battle, and he proved unable to open the shells. Eventually, he seemed to solve the problem by relaying the clam to his den, where I presume he got assistance from his family. Timmy looked like a toy fire engine racing back and forth from the clam flats to his den.

As I watched the bears at work, I was impressed by the dexterity of their paws and connecting claws. A bear relies upon them for walking, running, climbing, swimming, digging, killing, feeding, lifting, raking, sensing, and self-defense. The bottoms of their paws are covered with a dark, double-thick pad that is shed during hibernation. The hind paws are larger than the front, but the front claws, which extend from two to five inches, are considerably larger than the claws on the back feet. The claws are made of kerotin, just like human fingernails. They are dark, but can whiten with age.

Bears walk flat-footed and are somewhat pigeon-toed, and both front and back limbs on each side work together for locomotion. This gives them a cute, but clumsy, appearance—which is dangerously misleading. Bears are fast and agile: Grizzlies have been clocked at 41 miles per hour in Denali National Park, Alaska, and brown grizzlies can run a 100-meter dash in 5.85 seconds from a standing start. Once, after watching a couple of bears chasing one another, I measured the distance between the prints made by one of the bears. They were 15 to 20 feet apart.

A storm blew in at the end of the first week and hung around for thirty-six hours. It was more annoying than dangerous, dropping the temperature into the forties and pinning me inside my tent. The bears themselves had little use for rain, and most hunkered down in their beds to wait it out. I felt kind of sorry for them—even though they're wild animals with thick coats designed for such weather. The resourceful bears dug their daybeds against the base of a hill, effectively blocking the wind, or tunneled under massive logs, concocting primitive shelters.

The storm gave way to one of the best days I have ever had in the Sanctuary. Warren was out on the tide flat pursuing his new heartthrob, Dahlia, a cute, compact blond of about 400 pounds. Dahlia was about half the size of Warren, who appeared to be as big as a steer. Unfortunately for Warren, Dahlia still had her two-year-old daughter Maggy with her. Warren had a habit of chasing difficult females. He did the same thing the year before with an unreceptive bear named Stephanie. Dahlia and Stephanie had two things in common: They enjoyed clamming, but they didn't enjoy Warren. Eventually, Warren usually wore the females down and had his way. That's what reminded me of my human friend Warren Queeney: They're both good-looking, persistent, and usually get their girls.

Generally, Warren is too busy chasing females to pay much attention to me, so I can observe him safely. Today was a little different. Warren was casually napping close to Dahlia's clam digging, when Timmy the Fox came by, woke him up, and pissed him off. Warren tensed up, signaling a low level of stress with a yawn. Timmy scurried over to Dahlia, starting her moving in my direction. Dahlia stopped near me and started to dig. Warren had had enough. His main objective that day was to have sex with Dahlia. He began stalking in my direction, treating me like a rival bear.

Warren's head was lowered and his ears were back, two major signals of an aggressive bear likely to charge. Timmy the Fox cowered behind my legs. "Aw, for crying out loud, Timmy! Now you've got me in a fine mess."

I had seconds to defuse the situation. Warren was a large bear, 1,000 pounds and 9 feet long. I spoke softly and calmly to him as he closed to within forty feet. Backing up slowly, I moved my head to one side to expose my neck, and lowered my eyes. This was the equivalent of the shaking of hands between two human fighters.

"Easy, Warren, easy, big boy. I'm not a problem," I said. Thirty feet from me, Warren finally started to slow down. He began to calm down, looking at Dahlia. Without running or turning my back on him, I retreated. Two minutes later, I was back on the grassy fringe above the beach.

The encounter had a profound effect on me. Though I had known Warren for over five years, I could have been killed. The lesson was clear: To live near mating grizzlies, I would have to be wary and respectful at all times.

The evening of my tenth day in the Grizzly Sanctuary was overwhelmingly beautiful. Most of the region's mosquitoes were still larvae, giving me a reprieve from the winged demons. The clear blue sky was reflected in the Sanctuary's creeks, ponds, and bays as brilliant turquoises, emeralds, and violets. Perhaps one day I'll have the chance to thank the creator of this splendor. Until then, I'll thank the bears.

At eleven-thirty P.M. things changed. The weather stayed gorgeous, but there was an odd feeling in the air. I poked my head out of the front tent flaps. There was Hulk, stalking toward my tent. He was without his mate, Daisy, and that concerned me. Did Tar win her back? My hope was that he would stroll by and pay me no mind, but Hulk stepped up on the raised dry ground and headed for the tent.

He closed to within twenty-five feet. Up close, his head looked bigger than a bushel basket. He was over four feet tall on all fours, and eight to ten feet long, nose to rump. With one swat he could kill me, and with another destroy all of my gear. My mind raced through my choices. I could withdraw, and try to hide in the woods; I could play dead; or I could confront him.

I had only one choice: to remain strong. Hulk's body language said attack: His ears were back, small slobber dripped from his jowls, and his eyelids were retracted back to reveal the yellow sclera. I wanted to scream, to curse, to use my street-fighting techniques, but it was a bear I was facing. I needed to convince both of us that I was a worthy bear: I broadened my shoulders and said, "Hulk, how can I help you if you want to hurt me? You are the champion, but I'll be yours if you let me live."

Hulk blinked, then he turned his head to one side and his aggressive signals evaporated. He then turned and waddled away into the Big Green.

Ten minutes after the incident, Daisy walked out onto the Big Green and intercepted Hulk, who began kissing and nuzzling her. They began caressing each other with their muzzles while rubbing and grinding their bodies together. It was quite beautiful. Minutes into their foreplay, Hulk mounted Daisy from behind, and began heated sex. It was only twenty minutes after our encounter. I may have been totally shaken, but the confrontation was no longer of any consequence to Hulk. Two hours later, while Hulk and Daisy rested together, I still couldn't sleep. During the rest of Hulk and Daisy's courtship, they mated closer and closer to my tent.

A Cessna 206 buzzed overhead, shattering the calm morning in the Grizzly Sanctuary. My friend Bill had flown in to bring me necessary supplies. Bill was perhaps fifty, tall and well built with thick, short-cropped hair. He owned an expensive fishing lodge many miles from the Sanctuary. Even though his lodge was far away, Bill occasionally flew by with clients on fishing expeditions.

I met him one year when he stopped by the Grizzly Sanctuary in search of halibut. A sort of born-again bear lover, Bill was intrigued by my work, and offered to stop by with supplies during my expeditions. I'd heard that he was once a bear hunting guide, but now he just photographs the bears. Bill's natural landing strip was a mile from my camp, so I grabbed my camera and quickly jogged the distance to his plane.

"Well, I see that you're not a pile of bones from those bears yet," Bill said, shaking my hand heartily.

"Not yet, but Hulk paid me a visit last night and it did get a little scary!"

"Well, heck, Timothy," he drawled. "I told you that for the most part, they're good bears, but it only takes one bad apple to wreck your day. You're probably finding that you have to sleep in the day, and fend off the curious visitors at night."

"I'm averaging two to four visits a night, Bill," I said. "Most just huff and blow by, but it's those cozier visits that really spook me. If it keeps up, I might have to move my tent to a quieter area."

"Yeah, Timothy, you might be better off moving back to that scrubby field. I've been flying over bear country for more than thirty years, and haven't seen a single person try to do what you are doing," Bill said. "Oh, a couple of years back there were some federal people doing a study a few bays north of here, but they nearly went bonkers from fear," he said with a smirk. "They had an electrified fence around their tents and were blowing off firecrackers and guns at all hours. They were petrified of the bears. They ended up running back to the safety of Washington, D.C.," he said and chuckled.

"Gosh, they were fools," I said and laughed. "This place is much safer than the capital!"

Just then, a young blond subadult bear appeared along the beach near the plane. He was playing with logs and a washed-up buoy.

"Well, ain't he a silly son of a bitch," Bill said. "Got a beautiful coat, too."

I snapped some photographs of the youngster. He certainly seemed familiar, but I just couldn't place him. Bill and I had just commented on what a nice, entertaining bear he was when he suddenly started pushing us. A cat-and-mouse game of tag went on between the bear and Bill and me. As the young bear charged us, we repelled him with stomps and shouts. Then Bill realized who he was.

"That's no nice bear!" Bill yelled. "That's Cupcake!"

I couldn't believe it was Cupcake. I hadn't seen Cupcake since he'd charged me the year before, but Bill had told me about him on several occasions. Cupcake was in the habit of charging Bill when he touched down in the Grizzly Sanctuary. During the winter away from the bears, Bill and I often discussed our hope that Cupcake's mother, LuLu, would finally cast him off, and that Cupcake would leave the Sanctuary. Yet here he was again this year, bigger and bolder than ever. He had momentarily stopped his charge, but eyed us from a distance.

"Lucky LuLu," I said to Bill. "She has a new family, and we're stuck with Cupcake."

"Wrong, Timothy," Bill said and laughed. "I'm not stuck with Cupcake. I'm flying to a warm, cozy lodge a hundred miles away from this devil."

Of all of the bears in the Sanctuary, the only one that really scared me was Cupcake. The Cake could ruin my expedition. Just to be safe, we chased Cupcake as far away from my camp as possible.

"You're worried, aren't you?" Bill asked.

"Yeah. Cupcake is a nightmare," I said sadly.

Bill pulled some supplies from his plane. "I'm out of here!" he yelled, firing up the Cessna. "I'll bring you and your friend Cupcake some groceries three days from now come Tuesday," he shouted over the roar of the engine.

"Thank you, Bill. I would be lost without you!" I shouted back. Bill took off, and I rushed back to my camp, hoping that Cupcake wouldn't follow.

A couple of hours after Bill departed, another plane buzzed the Sanctuary. It circled both the Big Green and the Playpen, then touched down on its floats in the center creek. Concerned for the safety of the bears, I grabbed my binoculars and ran to the creek.

The plane's engine coughed and sputtered as it maneuvered for a position to beach along the creek. I had found a spot that allowed me to view the activity without being seen, but Timmy the Fox didn't care who saw him. "Aw, for crying out loud, Timmy!" I called to the fox as he sprinted from the brush. "Stay down low, buddy."

The plane was a seven-seat DeHavilland Beaver. I zeroed in with the binoculars and saw six people. Most carried large cameras and tripods, and it was obvious to me what they were up to: Eco-tourism had found its way to the Grizzly Sanctuary.

I had mixed emotions about bear-viewing tours. On the positive side, the increasing number of nonviolent tourists has pumped millions of dollars into the Alaskan economy, proving that living bears are a beneficial, not to mention renewable, resource. The operators generally charge $300 to $400 per person for a half-day excursion. They're modeled after the popular whale-watching trips that have thrilled people for years and have helped to increase an awareness of endangered species. The downside is that these people, though they mean well, can also hurt the animals they've come to see. In many places, migrating gray whales have radically altered their courses to avoid the sightseers. Similarly, some bears have been driven to less productive habitats to avoid the planes. I've also witnessed overzealous photographers getting way too close to non-threatening bears, which interrupts the animal's feeding habits.

As I watched, one of the bears they were photographing approached the group. Unfortunately, it was Cupcake. He calmly came closer, than suddenly charged. In an instant, cameras and tripods crashed to the ground. A barrage of whistles, horns, and firecrackers screamed throughout the Sanctuary. The eco-tourists bolted for the safety of the plane. Within seconds the plane had lifted off from the creek. Cupcake had temporarily put a halt to bear viewing in the Grizzly Sanctuary.

Unfortunately, for me that wasn't the end of the incident. Cupcake decided to move back to the Big Green. Through my binoculars, I could see Cupcake's silly blond head bouncing toward me. "Darn it! Darn it! Darn it!" I shouted. "Time to scatter, little fox!" I scurried back to camp, wishing for a miracle.

Back at the tent, I wrote about my Cupcake paranoia. Fifteen minutes into it, I peeked outside. Not 100 yards away bobbed Cup-fucking-cake! Like Dennis the Menace, he looked sweet and innocent with his blond mane flapping in the wind. Unlike Dennis, Cupcake was 300 pounds of muscle, claws, and teeth. I was both frightened and humiliated: With all of the huge monster grizzlies around, I had to be stalked by the puniest one.

Then a ray of hope appeared. Big Mr. Chocolate started heading toward Cupcake. Now, my old friend Mr. Chocolate was easily 1,000 pounds, and Cupcake looked like a cub in comparison to his bulk. Poor Cupcake pissed himself at the sight of Mr. C., and ran off at a gallop. Eventually, the Cake stopped far away in a less productive area of the Big Green. Although a safe distance from me, he was still within sight of my tent. I went out and thanked Mr. Chocolate, but he ignored me and went back to his sedge grass salad.

The night passed quietly, with not even a peep out of Cupcake. In the morning, I could tell that there had been a major change in the Big Green. (I call it the Big Green not only for its vast sedge pastures, but also for the size of the inhabitants that take over each June.) As I surveyed the Big Green, I couldn't believe my eyes: The nearby field was packed with 1,000-pound grizzlies. There are few places on earth where bears this big remain, let alone gather in the open. Most really large grizzlies have been forced to become nocturnal because of trophy hunting and illegal poaching. The Sanctuary is one of the few places on earth where these huge bears can be active during the day and thus live the way nature intended.

I rushed through breakfast, anxious to be out among the giants of the Big Green: Mr. Chocolate, Monster, Warren, Hulk, and Hefty. Except for Warren, these bears were primarily here to harvest tons of sedge grass. Each year I knew when the sedge grass was at its maximum protein level because the very largest bears took over the Big Green.

Warren was eating sedge grass like the others, but his main passion this time of year was sex. He had finally succeeded in making Dahlia his mate. Fifty yards to Warren's right grazed Hulk and Daisy. They were still together. All of a sudden, the big bears began to move nervously, bowing their heads in submission. Warren herded Dahlia away in retreat, and Hulk did the same with Daisy, so I scanned the horizon to see what was coming. Czar, possibly the earth's largest living bear, was back: 5 feet high at the shoulder; 10 or 11 feet long from nose to butt; and at least 1,500 pounds. I hadn't seen Czar in nearly three years, and I was happy to see that he had survived the many human and natural dangers.

8

The parade of giant grizzlies continued into late June. As more large bears moved into the Big Green, most of the females and adolescents, including Cupcake, abandoned the area. I was happy to be rid of Cupcake for now, but the atmosphere in the Big Green was still very tense.

Bears of the Grizzly Sanctuary and other areas adhere to a social hierarchy. Among bears, size usually determines rank, but other factors, such as levels of aggression, play a distinct role. Generally, large adult males are at the top, mothers with cubs second, larger male adolescents third, and female adolescents and cubs are at the bottom. Usually the pecking order is clear, and the top of the ladder is occupied by one alpha male. However, in the Big Green so many large males competed for the top rung that no single male was able to dominate. Czar provided some stability, but he was rarely in the Big Green. For most of the season, the other large males jockeyed for the top spot, a competition that makes the Big Green a frightening place.

I hiked through an area thick with alder, pine, and a variety of sprouting plants. The vegetation grew wildly because of the plentiful rain and I could barely see in front of me. It was every camper's nightmare—walking through bear country without knowing what was ahead.

Generally, I used all of my senses to detect bears. Today, however, smell was useless because there were so many bears around that the air was perfumed with their scent. In wooded areas it's usually easy to hear bears approaching because they thrash through the brush like runaway trains, but the wind was deafening; it sounded like bears were everywhere. I was just going to have to rely on sight and intuition.

Just as I reached the edge of the Big Green, something big and brown stood up not ten feet away. The wind was in my face, so the bear didn't notice me. I crouched low and methodically cleansed the fear from my system. The bear was so close that I was almost knocked over when he stretched his foot toward me. Then he slowly lumbered forward, out into the Big Green. After he got a short way into the field, I got my camera and took a few photos. He heard the shutter and looked back through the woods, catching my eye. Looking in the bear's eyes, I realized that he was Garth. When I'd met him a few seasons before, he hadn't been this big. Now he was as big as a Buick, and aside from Czar, the largest bear in the area. Garth went to the nearby creek and drank some water, then promptly chased away two other large bears in a display of dominance. As long as Czar wasn't around, Garth had a chance to be the top male. Few humans ever get to witness the power struggle for dominance among grizzlies. This battle has been going on in the Grizzly Sanctuary for 40,000 years, over countless generations of bears. As Garth bullied his way around the Big Green, bears scattered everywhere. The tension was high in the field, and I decided to go back to my tent before I was run over.

I returned to my tent and got a shock. Mickey, a bear I had

known for many years, was dragging himself across the field. I had met Mickey the same summer I met Booble, and had watched him on the clam flats many times, peacefully coexisting with the others. Now his back limbs seemed to be useless. He moved like an elderly human in need of a walker. His condition crushed me, but I felt helpless. I have always believed in letting natural selection take its course. Nature may be cruel from moment to moment, but its overall effect is to create balance. However, Mickey's predicament forced me to find a compromise.

Mickey needed nourishment and rest, which was not possible with Garth, Monster, and the other giant bears in the area. I slowly reacquainted myself with Mickey, singing soft, gentle songs of love and praise. I herded him in the direction of the nutritious grass near my tent. He didn't seem nervous, and at my prodding slowly dragged himself onto the sedge grass. Mickey began to feed while I stood guard. I left him alone while keeping an eye out for any intruders. If larger bears attempted to dominate Mickey, I stepped out and calmly dissuaded them. After Mickey was sated, he curled up fifty feet from my tent and slept. Respectfully, I tiptoed around my camp for several days, monitoring Mickey's progress as he slowly regained his strength. Everything was going really well until Timmy the Fox wiggled into the brush to check out Mickey. Startled, Mickey picked up his head; it looked as if all of my work would be ruined by the orange devil. But for once, Timmy surprised me and lay down next to the injured bear. "Timmy, I've never been more proud of you!" I said to the silly creature.

As Mickey healed, I thought about my interference with nature. It was of little consequence to the Grizzly Sanctuary as a whole. But in my heart, it seemed right and felt good.

Mickey continued to recuperate, moving a bit more fluidly every day. He fed on the sedge grass, and at night slept safely near the tent. One day, as I was keeping an eye out for any bears that might bother Mickey, I noticed that Holly had settled in the woods surrounding my camp. I had met Holly and Mickey at the same time, when they were subadults clamming with Booble. Holly had her first cub with her. Given my history with Holly, I was thrilled to see her with her young, but her baby was obviously frail.

Holly looked good: plump, with clean, golden fur. The cub, however, was much smaller than others its age. Most cubs, even this early in the season, weighed twenty to twenty-five pounds. Holly's cub didn't look as if it weighed even ten pounds, despite the fact that it was solo. A cub without siblings should have been much heavier, benefiting from the lack of competition for mother's milk. The cub, Thumper, was deep brown, with dark dots for eyes and triangular ears. I was happy to have this tiny family move in so close to my tent.

It is important for growing cubs to play with one another. Play-fighting teaches communication skills through different forms of physical posturing and vocalization. All cubs love to play-fight, and many bears continue to do so for several years. It was a shame that baby Thumper didn't have any brothers or sisters. As Holly fed on sedge grass Thumper rolled, flipped, and twirled. I felt about Thumper the same way I had about Cupcake as a cub: I wished I could be his playmate so that he wouldn't be alone.

A few hours later, Hulk waltzed Daisy into the center of the Big Green and started having sex. It was a great opportunity for me to fill the holes in my educational presentations by getting photos of mating behavior. I got to within fifty feet, and set up my camera in a tall row of grass. The wind was in my face, suppressing my scent and keeping my position a secret.

I had shot almost a whole roll of film when the wind dropped and Hulk detected the rapid clicks of the shutter. Hulk seemed concerned that I was a rival bear and I was afraid that my presence would interrupt the important reproductive activity. I stood up and walked away from the grassy cover, waving to Hulk and wishing him well. Relieved that I was not competition, Hulk resumed sex with Daisy.

Most grizzly sexual encounters last about an hour, although I have observed ones that lasted as long as two hours. Today, Hulk and Daisy were finished in thirty-eight minutes. After Hulk climaxed, Daisy broke free and moved about twenty feet away. Hulk growled as he charged after Daisy to paw and caress her. They seemed so blissful. Suddenly, Hulk leaped up and turned around, walking toward me. Just as I started to panic, Hulk stopped at the spot where he and Daisy had had sex, and sniffed the ground; bears are an extremely scent-oriented species. Daisy caught up with Hulk, and nuzzled him lovingly. With just a touch of luck, I'd be right back here next year in the company of her new family.

That evening ended with a visit from a gentle subadult named Lazy, who more than lived up to his name. I retired to the tent, not the least bit concerned by Lazy's proximity.

The moments approaching dusk were one of my favorite times. At night over my AM radio I could receive an array of stations, from Anchorage to San Francisco. On rare evenings, I even received KNX news radio out of Los Angeles. It was bizarre to be in the middle of complete wilderness, listening to a traffic report from Southern California. My favorite program was *The Bruce Williams Show,* from Anchorage, Alaska. Mr. Williams was kind of like the Wizard of Oz, offering up advice and remedies for callers with all sorts of problems. I found him to be amazingly resourceful, and respectful of his audience. Often, I wondered what kind of remedy Bruce would offer for a 1,000-pound bear that wanted to come into your tent.

I stepped out of the tent to relieve myself. Snuggled against the tent, a bear peered up at me. Startled at first, I relaxed when I realized that it was Lazy. "Lazy, are you listening to the radio, too?" I asked. Lazy picked up his head and gazed toward me with sleepy eyes. "You can rest here if you absolutely promise not to wreck the tent," I told the bear like a concerned parent. Normally, I would shoo a bear away, but Lazy, with his head tucked under his paws, looked too comfortable. "Sleep tight, Lazy," I said, and we fell asleep listening to the KGO San Francisco *Ray Taliaferro* program.

The next morning, huffing, puffing, and jaw popping woke me. Half asleep, I stumbled out of my tent. A female bear was being pursued by a male I didn't recognize. "How about a little consideration, guys. It's not even seven A.M.!"

Despite the steady rain, the male bear continued his chase, then overcame the female and mounted her not 100 yards from the tent. Suddenly, Monster came over and wanted a piece of the action. Monster easily outweighed the other male by at least 200 pounds, but that didn't seem to matter. He completed his sexual act, then stood up to Monster's advances. As Monster crept away, I began to think that he could use some help with his self-esteem.

The minor yet pesky storm of the previous three days had finally begun to peter out. I had been resting, reading, and relaxing, but now it was time to get back to the bears. I was up and at 'em by eight A.M. I ate my usual hearty breakfast of a peanut butter and jelly sandwich, banana, and three chocolate Chips Ahoy cookies. After breakfast, I had to go to the bathroom. I usually performed this biological function far from the tent in fairly deep holes that I dug near the beach, since bears sometimes dig up and eat human waste for its salt and undigested components. The thought of that disgusted me, so I was careful to use less-traveled bear areas.

I walked through the pathway behind my tent, and stopped when I noticed a bear in a tide pond. The bear looked all too familiar. I peeked through the grass to get a better look, hoping I had mistaken the bear's identity. Cupcake. I was obviously going to have to wait.

I retreated in horror as Cupcake seemed to catch my scent and head right for me. Anticipating the worst, I grabbed a firm walking stick and my Counter Assault pepper spray from my tent. Just then, Cupcake appeared.

"Don't even think about it, Cupcake!" I shouted. "Just leave right now!" Cupcake circled around to the front of the tent and sat down on some logs just fifteen feet away. At first he just watched me. But his civility didn't last: Within minutes he was advancing toward me.

"Back, back!" I screamed. "Sit back down, Cupcake!" In that moment, I was more scared than I'd ever been. My previous incidents with Hulk, Monster, and Warren paled in comparison; the giant bears didn't frighten me nearly as much as Cupcake. He was the one bear in the Grizzly Sanctuary that made a habit of charging me. Cupcake's massive blond head was shining in the sun, and his deep, dark eyes were bright, sparkling with curiosity. I only had seconds to decide whether to spray him with the bear mace. If Cupcake's previous behavior was any indication, a friendly course of action would probably end in disaster.

Cupcake made the first move and rushed me vigorously, powerful paws tearing up the grass. I backed up against the tent. As he closed the final five feet, I blasted him with a solid burst of Counter Assault pepper spray. A toxic orange cloud collected on his face, blinding him momentarily. Cupcake spun and withdrew, galloping to the closest field. He coughed in agony, rolling his head in the grass. I was beside myself, miserable at being responsible for Cupcake's suffering. I called to Cupcake, almost crying. "I'm sorry, Cake! You scared me!"

Cupcake's reaction to my apology was to charge at me full steam. He made a beeline right for the tent, his snout covered in orange bear spray. "Back!" I yelled, letting loose another volley of Counter Assault. The spray alone was not enough to deter the bear. I ran toward Cupcake screaming and waving the walking stick like a propeller. Cupcake ran for his life. I chased him through two creeks, ranting and raving as I swung the stick behind him. A dozen or more grizzlies picked up their heads at the spectacle. From across the Big Green, Cupcake appeared to be defeated. As I departed, Cupcake washed himself in the creek, trying to rinse the stinging chemicals from his fur.

I was no longer sorry I'd sprayed Cupcake. Other people occasionally enter the Grizzly Sanctuary, and even though it is illegal, most carry guns. Giving him a dose of fear was exactly what he needed for his own survival. I sincerely hoped to know Cupcake for a very long time. Healthy bears can live to thirty years in the wild, and the thought of knowing the Cake when I was sixty made me smile. Maybe then, he would finally let me be.

Back at the tent I saw Mickey, asleep in the grass. I was surprised that the raucous incident with Cupcake hadn't disturbed him, and was glad that he was still safe. I looked around for Timmy the Fox, knowing how much he loved action. Sure enough, I found him sprawled out on my green jacket. Two fresh, gray turds soiled the lining. The morning joust with Cupcake must have scared the crap out of him. Not angry in the least, I patted him on the head and set him up with a bed of clean clothes. Then I headed to the ocean to wash up. Instead of staying behind, Timmy followed. After the upsetting incident with Cupcake, it felt good to have such a loyal friend.

As we approached the ocean, Holly and Thumper were running along the tide line. Thumper looked much healthier, at least ten pounds heavier than the last time I'd seen him. As a matter of fact, Thumper looked like a well-fed infant. It seemed that Holly was a capable mother, and that Thumper had a real chance of making it.

The key to successfully nourishing a baby bear like Thumper is mother's milk. A bear's milk averages 33 percent fat, 11 percent protein, and barely 10 percent carbohydrate. In contrast, a human's milk contains only 3.5 percent fat. Young grizzlies usually nurse for at least a year and a half, though they begin to eat other foods after six months. Not all bears stop nursing then; for example, Cupcake had still been nursing at two and a half. Between LuLu's milk and the other available foods, Cupcake had looked like a stuffed piñata when he was young.

A spring cub like Thumper ought to weigh about fifty-five to eighty pounds at six months. Since most cubs are born in January or February, Thumper was most likely five months old. Thumper was not quite twenty pounds, which meant that Holly had her work cut out for her to bring this baby up to proper grizzly specifications.

Timmy the Fox ran up to Thumper and pecked at his tiny snout. Thumper bounced with excitement, and chased Timmy across the beach. Holly huffed until Thumper returned to her side, then the two continued down the beach.

I wanted to sleep late the next morning, but as usual in the Grizzly Sanctuary, my plan was altered by the bears. A pair of hyperactive subadults were playing tag in my camp, noisily knocking over a tripod and sending it flying. The subadults' behavior was nothing personal, but it signaled a change in the Grizzly Sanctuary.

The obnoxious subadults who stampeded my camp were among the last arrivals to the Grizzly Sanctuary that season. The bears trickle in from late May through early June, and reach their maximum count near the summer solstice. At first they maintain large personal spaces between each other. Eventually, as more bears migrate into the Sanctuary, they must learn to tolerate their fellow grizzlies in order to eat as much food as possible before winter. Those that cannot adapt leave. The amount of animals a given habitat can support is called its carrying capacity, and the Grizzly Sanctuary has one of the highest carrying capacities for bears in the entire world. At its peak season, there are well over 100 grizzlies in the Sanctuary.

As the subadults Rowdy and Chance continued to wrestle

around my camp, I used the opportunity to get some photographs. At three years of age, male bears average 300 to 425 pounds, and these two were prime examples. Standing on their hind legs, they collided, pawing and biting.

Many bear biology experts claim that important forms of communication are learned from play-fighting, though it can often get quite rough. When Rowdy drew blood, Chance decided it was time for a dip in the local creek. Deprived of a partner, Rowdy approached me: Apparently, I was to be his next victim. Turning my back would surely have invited a serious charge, so I backed slowly away. Once again, I was in a dangerous situation with a subadult. I needed to come up with a strategy to deal with Rowdy and, when I spotted my old friend Mr. Chocolate grazing in the field, I knew what to do. I angled back toward him, and as Rowdy got to within twenty feet of me, he suddenly caught sight of the immense Mr. Chocolate. Rowdy had committed a major sin among grizzlies: Never interfere with the feeding of a dominant bear. Mr. Chocolate's ears snapped back and he exploded toward the subadult. Rowdy's confident demeanor immediately changed to fear and he fled back to his best friend, Chance. I sat down in relief, safe with Mr. Chocolate.

After many years, I'm pretty competent at reading bear signals. I have to be, because my life depends on it. So when I saw a new male about seven years old and not quite full grown at 650 pounds, I took a good look at his body language. At first, I thought that the bear was mildly startled by my appearance, and wanted to get a better look at me. I knew that he would also use his sense of smell to get a complete picture. By his docile gestures, I guessed that he was going to run away. His ears were up and his fur was flat, with no chomping or head shakes. But this time, my interpretation was wrong, and he suddenly turned from docile to aggressive. He moved directly for me, head lowered and ears back, signals of aggression, and once again, I was in trouble. I looked around, hoping that Mr. Chocolate would be able to rescue me, but he was grazing almost a quarter of a mile away. Only Cupcake was close enough to help, but that was completely out of the question, since there was no way this bear was going to defer to the Cake. The bear was only seconds away from a full charge. Swallowing my fear, I began to snarl and hiss, charging and kicking up mud. As I got closer, his anger dissipated and he became submissive. Without running, he quickly moved into the Big Green and started to graze. In aggressive bear encounters, most of the time a good bluff wins. I marched past the bear and turned my back on him, displaying a signal of dominance. Now that I had the chance to take a more leisurely look at him, I could see that the big brown bear had a short buzz-cut military look to him, so I named him Sergeant Brown. When I returned an hour later, Sergeant Brown respected me, like a good soldier.

The next afternoon brought Hulk and Daisy by for another rendezvous near my tent. Daisy led Hulk in a slow parade across the Big Green, stopping about fifty feet from the tent. Then Hulk mounted his lover and began the ancient dance of procreation. Why had this pair of wild grizzlies chosen to have sex directly in front of me? I had been sitting or standing in plain view as they marched toward me, while the wind had surely carried my scent to their keen nostrils. For some reason, Hulk and Daisy didn't mind my company. Perhaps at this point, three weeks into the expedition, I had proven that I wasn't a threat. Things were starting to settle down for me in the Grizzly Sanctuary. While difficult bear encounters in the immediate vicinity of my tent still occurred, they were no longer three to five a night, but one or two a week.

The majority of brown grizzlies now accepted me, and casually let me within their personal space at any hour of the day. I was honored, and really felt like a grizzly.

Later that evening, I hiked through a good portion of the Grizzly Sanctuary. Without even looking into the Playpen, I saw fifty-two bears. Without a doubt, there were many more bears in the Playpen, as well as simply out of sight on the Big Green. A total population of perhaps two hundred bears would not have surprised me, and I was the only human in the Grizzly Sanctuary. The Sanctuary was truly an amazing place.

Around ten P.M. the winds began to howl from the east. Eastern winds usually meant rain in the Grizzly Sanctuary. I've learned that winds from the southeast cause the worst storms, generated by counterclockwise spinning low-pressure subsystems. On the other hand, winds out of the north and west generally brought sunny conditions, caused by clockwise high-pressure systems. A marine forecast over the radio confirmed building gale-force winds; I knew that rain could not be far behind.

As the winds increased, I fell asleep. Like many nights on the Big Green, this one was interrupted by the presence of an animal outside my tent. As I prepared to do the yell, dive, and shoo drill once again, I wondered who would be foolish enough to go out in the storm. Sticking my head out in the rain, I braced myself for the worst, but there was nothing. No half-ton male, no gang of subadults. Most important, no Cupcake. Suddenly, a familiar flash of red solved the mystery. Timmy darted inside the front vestibule awning of the tent and curled up. "What's the matter, boy, the wind scaring you?" I combed his mottled orange and white fur and told him a bedtime story about a good fox. I thought about letting him into the tent proper, but I knew that Timmy would spend the night rummaging through my possessions and leaving his signature crap. He would have to sleep in the vestibule. In the morning, Timmy the Fox had departed, but not before leaving a stinking dump on my hiking shoes. "Aw, for crying out loud, Timmy!" I yelled into the rain. "Is this the thanks I get for giving you shelter?"

The storm was easily the most powerful of Expedition '95. My first priority was to ensure the safety of my camera gear, and I quickly stored the delicate equipment in waterproof bags. The sleeping bag was already damp, so I lined the floor with trash bags. Then I went out and put a layer of trash bags between the fly and the tent. The tent was beginning to pull loose from its moorings, and as the cold wind and rain pelted my face, I heaved large logs on each corner, effectively solving the magic carpet syndrome. As I climbed back inside, Mr. Chocolate caught my eye. He was taking advantage of the rain-fed sedge grass growth and the near bearless greens. "Hi, Mr. Chocolate," I called. "I'm glad you're having a good day. This rain is really beating up my tent. If it keeps up, I may have to join you outside." Mr. Chocolate looked up momentarily, then went back to the harvest. It was just one of countless storms the great bear would have to endure over a lifetime. I climbed back into the tent, safe and secure.

9

I was trapped in the tent for several days by the rain. Finally, after what seemed like an eternity, the rain let up a bit. The radical low tides were back, and I was anxious to return to the flats. A safe distance from the tent, I ate a breakfast of PB and J, cookies, a banana, and some vitamins, and washed it down with one of my last five cans of Coca-Cola. As soon as I stepped from the tent, I could see Mickey. He was still damp from the storm, but actually moving around stiffly on all four legs, and I was suddenly hopeful that he would be able to heal completely. Holly and Thumper were nearby, eating the sedge grass. "Good morning, little family, are you on your way to the low tides to dig some clams?" I asked. "Hope to see you there," I called, and headed for the beach. Sure enough, Holly and Thumper tagged along, following me to the flats.

Holly dug right in and extracted a series of razorback clams in quick succession. Thumper had little interest in trying to copy his mother. Instead, he explored, ran in circles and stumbled around, too captivated by the world at large to focus his limited attention span on clams. Occasionally, he tried to snatch a clam from his mother. Most mother bears feed their cubs only milk, so it's up to each individual cub to round out his or her diet with solid food.

Stealing from the mother is a common tactic. Thumper wasn't much of a clammer, but he was a respectable thief. He darted between his mother's legs, grabbed a clam, and ran away. Holly relaxed and let her cub get away with the robbery.

Speaking of thieves, Timmy the Fox quickly joined the session. Thumper could've learned a thing or two from him. When Timmy wasn't trying to dig his own clams, he was slipping in and out of the group of bears, stealing from anyone who blinked. At times, the bears would go after him, but he was too quick to be caught. Fortunately, Timmy spent more time clamming than stealing. First, he'd locate a clam by spotting the tiny air holes. Then, he'd hunch over the spot and dig in a furious windmill fashion. Beach sand would fly into the air while he disappeared into the deepening hole. Eventually, the only part of Timmy I would be able to see would be his silly orange tail. Invariably, he'd pop out of the hole with a clam the size of his head clenched in his teeth. Timmy had finally learned how to open the shell, assaulting the clam like a woodpecker. After licking the shell clean, Timmy bounced over to me.

"Congratulations, Timmy," I said sarcastically. "You're the greatest fox in the whole world!"

After finishing his meal, Timmy took a break and skipped over to Holly and Thumper. Thumper started chasing Timmy around Holly. A game of cat and mouse developed between the cub and the fox. Timmy scooted by Thumper's nose, with Thumper in hot pursuit. Eventually, Timmy tired of the game and sought refuge behind my legs. Thumper charged halfway, thought better of it, and ran back to his mother.

Holly and Thumper were not the only mother-child pairs on the flats that day. Saturn, the five-year-old daughter of Beacon and

Comet, was there with her spring cub Wilcox. (Females, such as Booble, Holly, and Saturn, raise their cubs without the aid of the males.) I named Wilcox in honor of one of America's leading environmentalists, Louisa Wilcox. I'm sure she would be proud.

It appeared that Wilcox was a girl, but at five months I couldn't be certain. Wilcox was quite a bit larger than Thumper but, like Thumper, Wilcox couldn't care less about clamming. Saturn seemed to be better at procuring food, like clams, and consequently was a bit larger than Holly.

Watching Saturn and Wilcox reminded me that I hadn't seen Beacon in several years. I had once saved Beacon's life from illegal poachers. Was it possible that I had failed Beacon since, and that he had been murdered? I always kept an eye out for Beacon, hoping for his safe return.

I only saw a few other bears clamming, far away on the north side of the Sanctuary's beach. Most of the large males were absent. It's a trade-off of sorts, for large males usually intimidate mother bears with cubs into leaving. I love watching the mothers teaching cubs how to dig up clams. Holly, Saturn, and Booble were part of a heritage thousands of years old. I hoped that it would still exist in the next century.

We all abandoned the clam flats about the same time, traveling over the steep, sandy wall that divided the beach from the grass. The marshes and trees that lay beyond held over a hundred bears. Wolves, moose, lynx, wolverines, river otters, beavers, and, of course, foxes also inhabited the Sanctuary. I often saw otter and wolverine tracks, and even some moose prints around my tent, but I rarely saw the animals themselves. The grizzly bears intimidated other animals into being secretive—except for foxes, of course.

I returned to the tent. Nearby I could smell a bunch of overripe bananas that Bill had brought me. I panicked—imagine how well the bears could smell the food. I scarfed down the barely acceptable parts, and tossed the rest of the fruit and the peels into a plastic bag. I needed to get rid of the rotting bananas, so I hiked back to the ocean to dispose of the fruit. After tossing what was left of the bananas into the water, I rinsed the bag thoroughly and tucked it into my pocket, careful not to litter in the Grizzly Sanctuary.

Returning to my camp, I stumbled upon a pair of two-year-old bear siblings hard at play. A perfect fringe of camouflaging alders hid me from sight while the wind blew my scent away from the bears. The twin males, about 300 pounds each, had lush coats of silver-tipped fur that gave them the classic, Rocky Mountain grizzly look. Because they were totally indistinguishable I named them Tommy and Tom, or the Thompson Twins.

While setting up my camera, a serious fight broke out between the twins. They leaped, growled, lunged, and hurtled themselves at each other. Then, unlike Rowdy and Chance, they separated to cool down. Fighting and playing styles differed dramatically from bear to bear, depending on each bear's personality.

I loved the moments like these with the Thompsons. They gave me the opportunity to fully use all of my camera gear. After all, besides trying to be a grizzly, and an environmental educator, I was also a photographer.

I had one minor concern about the Thompsons: They had been playing just a hundred yards from my tent. Subadults are the biggest danger to my expedition because subadults, just like human adolescents, are likely to challenge the world around them. I hoped that the Thompson Twins wouldn't be too mischievous.

After the Thompson interlude, I ate my dinner a safe distance from the tent. At least two out of three meals a day were peanut butter and jelly sandwiches. After a month in the wild, I'll admit it: I was craving some serious human food. I rarely eat red meat, but the thought of a double-decker cheeseburger had me salivating. Sure enough, that night my radio picked up nothing but food commercials. In Anchorage, it was all-you-could-eat racks of baby-back ribs at Tony Roma's. In San Francisco, an Italian restaurant advertised rich, delicious pasta, all thoughtfully prepared by Chef Luigi. Meanwhile, I ate a stale Ritz cracker and dreamed of bursting into that Italian restaurant on San Francisco's Fisherman's Wharf with Czar, Hulk, and Mr. Chocolate.

"It's all you can eat tonight for me and the boys!" I would say. Czar inhaled thirty-three orders of hearty lasagne as fast as the waiters could whip them out, while the staff tossed gourmet pizzas into Mr. Chocolate's open mouth, shiitake mushrooms and goat cheese flying. Hulk would display a bit of class, escorting his girlfriend Daisy to a quiet corner booth. Then Hulk, with a tablecloth under his chin, would order trash pails of angel-hair pasta in a creamy garlic Alfredo sauce, followed by the restaurant's entire rare wine collection. "Just think," I would say to the cook, "our visit is all a result of your radio commercial!"

Tormented by the radio, I stepped outside. The Thompson Twins were nearby, grazing on sedge grass. A few steps away, Cupcake grazed as well. I was completely confused. The day before, the field held a dozen half-ton grizzlies. Now, one of the most productive sedge grass fields was being dominated by three overactive subadults and Timmy the Fox. I shook my head. "Good night. Try to leave a little of the Sanctuary intact!" With that, I turned in and slept soundly until a fierce new rainstorm hit the Grizzly Sanctuary.

There are no specific weather reports for the Grizzly Sanctuary. The closest general forecast is for large bodies of water in Alaska. Hearing of moderate winds from the northeast, I expected nothing more than showers. But the winds were really starting to blow, and there were already two inches of water in my rain gauge. Years before, when I first met Czar, there had been an eleven-day storm in which rain fell in buckets, filling my five-inch rain gauge every two days. This storm was strong but, thankfully, not as powerful as that one.

At six P.M., boredom and hunger combined to force me out of

the tent and into the cold rain. While I was waiting for some water to boil on the portable stove, I saw a gathering of buffalo-sized bears on the Green. I turned off my stove and headed over. One of the large males stepped out of the brush, a safe distance away. I couldn't recognize him because the rain had matted his hair. The bear's head was down and his ears were pulled back—I thought at first that he'd picked up my scent and was coming after me. I started to retreat, then noticed that the bear was performing the "Cowboy Walk."[9] Males sometimes perform this odd, stiff, bow-legged shuffle during confrontations with other males. I was pretty sure that I hadn't provoked the Cowboy Walk, so I ducked down and waited. Sure enough, big Garth thundered into view. No amount of rain could disguise that mammoth. Garth was also doing the Cowboy Walk, and with at least 200 pounds on the first bear, Garth, clearly the big gun, had the advantage.

Instead of fighting, the pair did a Texas two-step, and the challenger backed down. Garth promptly took over the other bear's sedge grass patch. After the tension lessened, I walked out into the field to get a fix on what was going on. Garth gave me a casual look, and I realized that he'd known I was there all along; Garth didn't get to be an alpha bear by ignoring his surroundings. With the other bear a safe distance away, he settled down and began eating. I realized that the other bear was Tar. Poor Tar. He always seemed to get the short end of the stick.

Looking more closely at the bears on the field, I saw why Garth had displaced Tar. Czar was back and had, no doubt, forced Garth to move. Like falling dominoes, larger bears displaced the next. Czar was immense, at least twice the size of Tar.

On the way back to the campsite, I saw that Hulk and Daisy were sleeping in my camp. They had been mating for almost three weeks, which is unusual. Most bear experts consider two weeks the maximum, making Hulk and Daisy an exceptional pair.

Despite the rain and cold, I decided to go down to the creek in my swimsuit to bathe. I bathed and shaved in an ice-cold creek close to the tent. Windy, a large male with a dark-chocolate coat and long fur around his face, stood above me along the bank, just forty feet away. He had seen me do this for half a decade, and didn't even blink, continuing to graze. At eight years of age he already weighed more than 800 pounds. Windy was not very social, and generally stayed a good distance away from the other bears. Yet Windy seemed quite comfortable when I was close by. Over the years, Windy has become one of my favorites.

That night, I treated myself to a tuna fish sandwich and a cup of hot chocolate for dinner. It was my last little can of tuna. The sandwich reminded me of the many meals I've eaten with Jewel, my best friend and writing partner, and her dad, Ted. Ted and Jewel have made many contributions to my cause. Last year, when all of my funds ran out, they even put me up for two months. I've hoped that Jewel would come out during one of my expeditions, but she's always been too frightened. She was right this time, for this trip would have had her terrified. She'll get out here someday, though.

The rain let up a bit, so I hiked over to the busy section of the Big Green. I settled into Garth's daybed, which had an excellent view of the fields. There were still a lot of bears out there. From Garth's bed, I could count twenty-two bears. By chance, a dozen of them had lined up so that I was able to get them all in one photograph. Czar was still around, looking bigger than ever. Even Warren made an appearance, although I didn't see his girlfriend Dahlia, and their courtship might well be over. Hulk stayed away from the group, hanging out near my tent—alone. I was very concerned. I ran to the tent to determine if Daisy had, in fact, left him. She was nowhere in sight, and Hulk seemed a little depressed.

I woke up a little depressed myself on the first of July, 1995. Another full day of rain, and my rations were growing smaller and staler. Because of the weather, Bill hadn't been able to make a supply drop for a week. I was afraid that he wouldn't be able to come until after the July fourth holidays. If the storm continued for weeks, which wasn't impossible in Alaska, I could starve.

"Get a grip, Timothy," I thought. "This is just the rainy-day, cabin-fever blues. It's nothing a bit of sunshine can't cure." The sun didn't show, but the rain let up enough for me to take a hike to the ocean. It was a small low tide, and only three unfamiliar bears were clamming. With both the tide and rain about to return, I decided to visit Timmy and Kathleen Fox. If they couldn't lift my spirits, nobody could.

The adults were absent, out working somewhere, but I knew that there were babies in the den. I still hadn't seen Timmy and Kathleen's litter. This was a perfect opportunity, but without their parents around, I was afraid that the little foxes would be too shy to come out. Around Timmy's den were the remains of past meals: bird parts, rodent skeletons, clamshells, fish bones, and even the remnants of a sea otter. Timmy the Fox and family may have been cute, but they were predators, and killed for survival. The bears were omnivorous, but with a diet of clams, plants, berries, and salmon, their level of violent predation was minimal compared to the foxes.

I sat in front of the sophisticated series of tunnels that comprised the den, hoping to get the attention of the pups below. I was just about to leave when a brownish-orange ball of fur popped out. It looked more like a kitten than a fox, all wide eyes and perky ears. After I took a few photographs, the rain began again. "You get back in that den before you catch cold," I said to the small fox. "If you get sick, Timmy will have my dead skeleton out here with the other remains! See you next sunshine, little baby." And off I trotted to my own den.

The Grizzly Sanctuary was really socked in with bad weather, and there was no way a plane could get through. A little more depressed, I heated up my last can of peas and carrots for dinner, along with two slices of very old bread and a miniature Three Musketeers candy bar. As far as remaining food went, I had a bit of candy, some Ritz crackers, a few pieces of stale bread, a small amount of peanut butter, and a Power Bar.

After my meager dinner, I strolled out into the rain to check on Hulk. He was all alone. Clearly, Daisy had left him. Hulk and Daisy's mating period had lasted twenty-two days. Before that, Daisy had mated with Tar for two full days. That made her period of estrous an astonishing twenty-four days. Yellowstone grizzlies had been observed to experience two distinct seven- to ten-day estrous cycles, separated by a brief period of anestrous, when the female is in heat.[10] Therefore, my documented observation of a single cycle lasting twenty-four days was exciting.

After Daisy's departure, Hulk spent all of his time revisiting the places they had been together. He lay down in the beds where they had slept, and sniffed the places where they had had sex. He was lethargic, and didn't eat much. Each time I checked on Hulk, the grass swished, just like an oncoming bear, and Hulk turned toward me, wide-eyed with anticipation. He was disappointed when it was only me. Hulk's eyes dimmed, his head dropped, and he resumed nibbling at the grass.

Sunday, July 2, was another miserable, drizzly, fog-shrouded day. This was last day I could have expected a visit from Bill. Things would be hectic over the holidays at his fishing lodge, so I couldn't expect him until Tuesday at the earliest. Mondays were out of the question, holiday or not. That was the changeover day at his place. A planeload of new customers would be flown in, then the old group would head out on the same plane.

At eight A.M., the radio delivered a double dose of bad news. A plane from the neighboring air service that brought me to the Sanctuary had crashed, killing the pilot and all aboard. It wasn't anyone I knew personally, but the flying community would nevertheless be crushed by the death of an associate and his customers. As for me, the subsequent FAA investigation could ground the airline, making it impossible for Bob or anyone else to pick me up. Even if they were allowed to fly on a limited basis, I was deep within one of the difficult-to-land danger zones that would almost certainly be ruled off limits. With my food supplies running out and the bad weather continuing, I was looking at some hard times.

The second bit of bad news was that a brown grizzly had killed a woman and one of her sons in the Chugach Mountains near Anchorage. The three were hiking on a national forest trail and ran into a grizzly eating a moose carcass. The bear probably thought they were after its food and defended the carrion, knocking one son down a steep hill, then killing the mother and second son. Such incidents add to "killer bear" hysteria, send rabid hunters out in waves, and make it harder for me to gain much needed sympathy for the animals. As with airline crashes, pro-bear PR has a hard time recovering after such violent incidents. But most of all, I was truly sorry for the family and friends of the victims. I hoped that they would all find room in their hearts for forgiveness. Whatever happened out there, I was reminded again of how quickly and efficiently a grizzly can kill. I'd only have to make one mistake and I'd meet with a similar fate.

Just as I was about to give up hope, Bill's plane flew out of the storm clouds and into the Grizzly Sanctuary. I sprinted the entire way to the plane, thrilled to see Bill. Even Timmy the Fox had a hard time keeping up with me.

"I see the bears haven't gotten you yet," Bill said, jumping from the plane. "Are you holding up OK?"

"I'm doing great, now that you're here. My food supplies are almost on empty," I said.

"Well, that storm chased me out of here for almost two weeks, but I got some bread, fruit, and assorted grub for you," Bill drawled. "I'm almost afraid to ask, but have you seen Cupcake?"

Booble as a 2½ year-old swimming across the center creek.

Timmy the Fox with two of his pups.

Czar, the undisputed ruler of the Sanctuary.

Beacon digging for clams at low tide on the flats.

Wilcox, Saturn's cub (and Beacon's grandson).

Hulk on the Big Green.

Hulk and Daisy mating.

The author with Thumper and Holly at the center creek.

Holly.

Thumper as a spring cub.

Mickey resting near the author's tent while recovering from his injuries.

Windy as a full-grown adult.

Booble as a four-year-old clamming on the flats.

Tar.

Rowdy and Chance play-wrestling.

Cupcake as a yearling.

Garth.

The Thompson Twins play-wrestling.

Monster, the scarred veteran of many battles.

Demon stalking the author.

Snowball catching salmon fry.

Freckles swimming back to shore with his salmon catch.

Freckles's hind paw—used for everything from running, climbing, and swimming to digging, lifting, and killing.

Molly demonstrating her superior salmon-catching skills.

Mr. Chocolate at the G Spot.

Molly among a flock of seagulls.

THE GRIZZLY SANCTUARY

The yearlings, Fresca and Ginger, with their mother, Booble.

"Unfortunately, I've seen too much of Cupcake. I thought that he was going to kill me last week; I had to blast him with the Counter Assault. Bill, it broke my heart to hurt him."

"Timothy, I've put in over thirty years living, fishing, and working around bears," Bill said, "and Cupcake's the worst of the lot. Don't feel bad about it."

"Well, at least he's been a pretty good bear since," I said.

"Yeah, well, don't count your chickens," Bill said. "I've got some people I'm going to take halibut fishing while the Pacific is calm," Bill added as we said our good-byes. "I'll try to see you in a few days."

"Bill, I just don't know how to thank you enough. I'd be lost— or very possibly dead—without you!" I said sincerely.

"Maybe I'll think of something later," Bill said, "but for now, I'm your ace in the hole. Until then, you just take care of yourself and the bears." Then he hopped aboard the plane and flew off.

I unpacked the goods and listened to the radio: The marine forecast called for winds from the northwest, which meant high pressure and beautiful weather. Sure enough, by early evening, the sun and wildflowers were out in the Grizzly Sanctuary. Kicking off my soggy shoes, I danced around in my bare feet. Twenty-seven bears grazed, dozed, and played around me. I moved among them at will, feeling like a bear myself. Wet, brown earth oozed and squirted between my toes.

Then I saw Hulk, all alone. I walked over to him and he stopped eating, raised his head, and stared blankly at me. Then his face became animated, and I felt a warm feeling flow toward me. He was sad now, but one day he would love again.

Chance the subadult bear chewed on sedge grass perhaps seventy-five yards from my tent. Rowdy, his brother, was not around. Cupcake was slowly making his way toward us. I was still wary of Cupcake, but he seemed to have his eye on Chance. Cupcake forged a deep creek, swimming effortlessly. Several minutes later, he invaded Chance's grassy pasture, slowly approaching the other subadult. At first Chance moved away, but then thought better of it and chased Cupcake back a few paces. Undeterred, Cupcake walked right up to Chance and gave him a playful swat. Chance accepted the challenge, and the pair began to wrestle. The level of play between Cupcake and Chance seemed much safer than combat with Rowdy. They were having a good time until Rowdy arrived and chased Cupcake away.

Cupcake was a lone cub like Thumper and Wilcox, and simply wanted to play. Perhaps all along, Cupcake had only wanted to play with me—maybe he'd charged and pushed me in fun. I did something a little bit risky. I walked back out in my bare feet through the woods toward Cupcake.

I talked softly to him, hoping he wouldn't run. I sat down on a fallen log and said, "I love you, Cupcake, I never meant to hurt you. You mean as much to me as any bear in the Sanctuary. You just want a friend, don't you?" Cupcake blinked at me, then sat down on the grass. "I hope you find your very own special friend. Good night, little fellow." I returned to my tent and got into bed, wishing all the animals good fortune and prosperity.

The rains returned the following afternoon, but they didn't pack as much punch as the previous storm had. I wandered out to the creek to refill my water jug carrying a full load of photography equipment just in case. One of the Thompsons ran out onto the Big Green on a large mud flat, scaring Holly and Thumper, who just happened to be cutting across the flat at the same time. Holly immediately herded Thumper toward me. The three of us cautiously passed Tommy Thompson and figured we were in the clear. But where there's one Thompson, there's sure to be another: Tom Thompson launched himself from a patch of bushes and charged right at Holly and me. Holly stood up on her hind legs like the Statue of Liberty, surprising Tom and slowing his charge. Then she turned and fled toward the beach with Thumper in tow. That left me there all alone. Next to a mother bear, I wasn't much of a threat. The Thompson Twins converged, rumbling toward me in a V formation. I screamed and charged at them. The Thompsons retreated and regrouped. For a fleeting moment, they seemed to be considering a second attack. Instead, they started play-fighting with each other and quickly forgot about me.

I, however, was left completely flustered and shaken. I settled myself, propped up the cameras, and calmed my trembling shutter finger enough to shoot some excellent photographs. After fifteen minutes, we headed in opposite directions with no hard feelings.

Concerned for Holly and Thumper, I wondered where they'd gone and if they were okay. A mother on the run like that can sometimes careen from one bad situation into another. I worried that they might have run into a truly dangerous situation. My anxiety was eased at two P.M. when Holly broke through the dense alders near my tent. I immediately fell to my knees so as not to intimidate her. "Hi, Holly! Hi, Thumper," I said. Mother and cub slowly walked over to the grass in front of my tent and started to graze. I snapped a few shots, but mostly let them be. After she'd had her fill, Holly rolled on to her back. Thumper climbed up and began to nurse, purring and bobbing from teat to teat.

After grazing some more, Holly and Thumper retired to a pile of logs near my camp and napped. Thumper lay under Holly's chin, tucked into her loving arms. They were out cold on the fallen timber; now I understood what sleeping like a log really meant. The sight of them sleeping made me drowsy, so I joined in. An hour later, we were all awakened by the rain. Hulk had left his daytime hideout and was grazing nearby. He slowly moved in Holly's direction, but she sensed that he wasn't a threat and remained in place. Usually, a male of Hulk's size terrified her, but today, Holly didn't act afraid at all. Hulk had remained lethargic, but had stopped sulking around all the places where he and Daisy had mated. "Atta boy!" I cheered. "There'll be another Daisy in your life."

Timmy the Fox stopped by with a mouthful of dead voles. Obviously, he had been out hunting for food for the family. Timmy raised a leg and squirted a friendly stream of urine to remind me that my campsite was his. Then he dropped a vole at my feet, and pranced away. "Thanks for the gift, little buddy!" I called out, one Timmy to another. I looked down at the small gray carcass and realized that if Bill hadn't stopped by with food supplies, this might have been my dinner. I took the dead vole out to the ocean and threw it into the water, looking around first to make sure that Chef Timmy the Fox wasn't around. It's never a good idea to insult the cook.

In between visits from Holly, Thumper, and Timmy the Fox, Mickey continued his convalescence. Mostly, he slept a short distance from the tent in a deep daybed that he had constructed. Occasionally, Mickey visited the sedge grass field nearby and ate the grass. Not only Mickey, Holly, and Thumper stayed near my camp; Lazy and Hulk were also only a stone's throw away. Luckily, Hulk never came close to my tent, so the situation remained peaceful. Just when I thought there wasn't any more room, Booble, Ginger, and Fresca showed up.

As we all sat around my tent, I heard the distant rumble of Bill's Cessna. I ran out of the tent and up the beach to greet him. Bill was accompanied by two of his lodge guests, Sara and Mac, from Georgia. They were on their way to a remote fishing spot, but Bill had thoughtfully stopped by to bring me some more food and a very important message.

"Hey, Timothy!" Bill said. "Bob will come by with his plane later today and take you to your next location."

I was suddenly sad, and Bill noticed the change. "Cheer up, son! It ain't like you'll be away from your bear family for long. Aren't you coming home to the Sanctuary later in the season?"

"Yes, I am. It's just that I'll miss them while I'm away!" I replied.

Sara and Mac proceeded to quiz me about my bear work. One thing for sure, I can talk the hind leg off the Holy Ghost when discussing bears. Fortunately, most of the people who ask find it interesting. I haven't actually met anyone who wanted to trade places, but at least they're entertained.

"Hey, let's quit yakking and go see some of the bears!" Bill cut in. Good thing he stopped me or they'd have missed the chance to fish, as well.

We cut across the sandy beach barrier and followed a bear path along the edge of the Sanctuary's largest tidal mud flat. We saw nearly twenty bears in one quick scan. Bill noticed Holly and Thumper eating some sedge grass, and I told the group about my close relationship with this little family.

"Let's go visit them," Bill said. "I bet they're the nicest bears in the wilderness."

Sara became anxious, questioning us about the potential danger of being close to a mother with her young.

"Sara," I said, "it's always imperative to respect mothers and cubs. So we'll give them at least a hundred yards of distance as a safety cushion." Sara nodded her head, but didn't look convinced.

"That's right," Bill added. "All bears have their personal distance at which they tolerate humans and other animals. Mother bears need the most room. When you get within a bear's zone, they might give you a little charge. Maybe a 'hop and stop' thingy. But the Momma bears do get a little more excited, and they'll smack you down if you happen to push it," he finished up seriously. Sara looked horrified.

"Oh, my!" she gasped. "Why don't we all get back in the plane and just go fishing?"

"Come on now, Sara," Bill said. "Let's just have a look-see! All's you gotta remember, Sara, is if a bear charges, there are four of us.

That means you don't have to win or place, just don't come in last!" Everyone laughed but Sara. Bill enjoyed his joke, but reminded everyone to absolutely never run from a bear.

As we edged closer, we were careful to leave a space of at least 100 yards between ourselves and Holly. Suddenly, a young male bounded into Holly's space, startling her. As usual, she came running right toward me. Only it wasn't just me this time. I was playing tour guide for some nice folks from the South. Holly kept barreling toward us. I'd seen this move so many times that I knew what would happen. Holly was going to use us as a buffer to shield her from the male. Sara and Mac, of course, had no idea what was going on. Sara cowered behind Bill, eyes wide with terror. Just as I'd thought, Holly passed within twenty feet, then veered off. I sang some songs to calm her down, and she quickly relaxed.

"That was a close one!" gasped Sara. "What happened to the hundred yards of personal space y'all were talking about?" she asked sarcastically.

"Well, Sara," Bill said, "out here in the wild you gotta take the cards as they come!"

Sara had had enough of bears for a lifetime. "Let's all go fishing before I have a heart attack!" she said.

We all walked down the beach, and the trio boarded the plane. "Now be careful when you leave here," Bill cautioned me from the cockpit. "Not all bears are as friendly as your pals in this Sanctuary. Good luck, Timothy, I'll see you in a month or so!" With that, he taxied the plane across the sand and took off.

After they left, I began running around frantically. It's amazing how fast the body starts moving when the time gets short. I only had a few hours remaining in the Grizzly Sanctuary, and a million things to do. Next stop: the Grizzly Maze.

I began with a glorious social call on Timmy the Fox's den. Once again, Tim was away, probably out gathering food for his thriving family. Six frisky pups had finally emerged, ransacking the immediate neighborhood. The tiny orange puffs ricocheted about like Ping-Pong balls out of control. Once in a while, a baby would actually stop moving, and eye me up and down with fascination. For the most part, they resembled a circus gone mad—they were certainly not threatened by my presence. Suddenly, the image of all of these orange maniacs on the loose in the Grizzly Sanctuary made me smile. Timmy the Fox and his family were just a few weeks away from creating mayhem in this wilderness. I left the pups, saying, "I'll be back in about a month, kids, so try not to wreck the place."

I tried to say good-bye to as many bears as possible, but they basically ignored me. I knew that mothers and cubs loved each other, and that bears like Hulk and Daisy clearly demonstrated deep bonds of affection, but it was probably too much to ask that they love me as well. My genuine sense of unconditional love for these animals was in itself my finest gift to them.

As I broke camp, a gray wolf wandered by me and my pile of outdoor gear. It was a gorgeous animal, a shimmering silver with black streaks through its coat and yellow eyes that seemed to glow in the daylight. I had never been so close to a wolf before. I said hello to it, and thanked the wolf for blessing me with its visit. It lingered for a few minutes, then loped off toward the glacier, running without concern in plain view of the bears. Then, in an instant, it vanished. I finished packing up my possessions. Except for the trampled grass around the campsite, I, like the wolf, left the wilderness without a trace.

10

I was ready to journey to the Grizzly Maze. The trip, via float plane, lasted no more than fifteen minutes, but it might as well have been a world away. As we sailed toward the Grizzly Maze, I was stunned once again by its beauty. The Maze consisted of two enormous freshwater lakes connected by a creek and surrounded by a vast, dense jungle of greenery. Fifteen-foot-high alders and spiny shrubs cloaked the floor of the Maze, creating a twisting thicket between the two lakes. The tangle would be absolutely impenetrable if not for the grizzlies that thrived in this environment. Over the centuries, the bears had carved an intricate series of tunnels through the landscape.

The circumferences of the tunnels were about the size of a large bear's body walking on all fours. The length of each tunnel varied, from a few feet to over a quarter of a mile. They were all one-way trails—the way the bear was going.

The Grizzly Maze didn't have sedge grass, clams, or many large game animals to attract the bears. Instead, flowing through its waters were the spawning salmon—an integral part of the diet of coastal brown bears. Several different species of salmon entered the wilderness lakes up a creek from a gateway ocean bay, to spawn in the freshwater creeks connecting the lakes. Bears came through the tunnels, then traveled out to the water's banks to catch the salmon. As far as I knew, no human had ever entered the Maze's tunnels to learn the ways of these grizzlies. I was determined to be the first.

I, however, had visited the Grizzly Maze twice before. I would have liked it even better than the Grizzly Sanctuary, but while I was there some of the bears almost killed me. It was so dangerous that I never so much as set foot in a tunnel. Instead, I set up camp far away from the tunnels, on a hill overlooking one of the creeks. It was one of the few areas in the Maze that was not enclosed by the alders.

The entire Grizzly Maze was encircled by mountains that guarded the beauty within. Only the narrow creek flowed in from the ocean.

Bob gently spiraled the steel-blue Beaver counterclockwise, down into one of the lakes in the Maze; I kind of felt as if I were being flushed down a toilet. The lake below shimmered, and I pointed out my desired drop zone to Bob. As he taxied toward the spot, he flung off his headset and gave me an earful.

"I don't mind telling you that I don't much like dropping you off here. Nobody camps back here, goddamn it! Not even the Eskimos set foot in this place." Bob paused momentarily, asking the Lord's forgiveness for taking His name in vain.

"Bob, I successfully camped back here before," I said.

"Yeah, and what happened? The bears tried to kill you!" Bob shouted.

"Oh, a couple got a bit frisky," I said.

"It only takes one, Timothy. Besides, you don't have that bear, what's his name, from the Sanctuary . . . uh . . . Uncle Chocolate, to look after you back here."

"His name is Mr. Chocolate, Bob. There's a couple of nice ones out here, too, like Taffy, Melissa, and old Quincy," I said, trying to calm Bob down.

"Nothing like Uncle Chocolate," Bob cut in. "I'm so wary of this place, I just wish I could fly him over here. Well, here's the deal—I'm lending you my thousand-dollar two-way radio, and this emergency signaling beacon while you're here. Back in town I asked around, and I was told that you never even carry any emergency communication devices," Bob said.

I looked the other way, feeling like a child caught red-handed. "I accept, Bob," I said, turning to look him in the eye. "Thanks so much for your concern."

"Well, at least we can unload nice and slow on this calm lake," Bob said. He looked around carefully at the panorama. "Seems a darn shame that one of the prettiest places in Alaska has to be the most dangerous."

"Actually, if all goes well, my next destination is the most dangerous," I said. "I've already made arrangements to get there by boat, because nobody will fly me in."

"Where in the name of the Holy Ghost could it possibly be worse than this jungle?" Bob asked.

"It's a place the Eskimos called the Forbidden Zone!" I said and told Bob its approximate location.

"I know that godforsaken place," he said. "You bet it's forbidden! I've even warned my pilots that landing near it will get them fired," he stressed. "I'm glad you booked a boat to pick you up from here and take you there, 'cause I would have felt bad telling you no. It's a nightmare to try to even land there, and if you do, the bears will kill you or run you out," he said.

"Well, we'll worry about that later," I said. "First, I'll have to survive the Maze."

Bob passed my bundles and boxes out of the back door of the plane. After stacking them up, he lingered for a few minutes, teaching me the ins and outs of the two-way radio. We tried to put off his departure as long as possible. But Bob needed to get going for his other scheduled flights. Climbing back on board, Bob had one last thing to say to me.

"The missus, me, and the kids will be doubling up on our prayers for you," he said sadly. "Plus, I'll fly by as often as possible, so be sure to check the radio when you hear me buzzing around." Bob looked around slowly, one last time. "It sure is pretty back here, but for some reason this place gives me the creeps. Please be extra careful, and God bless," he said.

"Thanks, Bob," I called to him as he taxied off. "I'll try to be careful. I really appreciate your making my work possible."

During the planning of Expedition '95 I spent many hours thinking about the appropriate spot to camp in the Grizzly Maze. I wanted a location that was dry and level and away from bear trails, tunnels, and their beds. I thought that the spot where Bob dropped me would be perfect. Soon after Bob took off, I discovered the error in my plan. First off, every spot that wasn't near a tunnel was next to a bear trail. In fact, the entire Grizzly Maze was either part of the grizzly trail system or a bedding area. I climbed higher up the side of a nearby mountain, looking for something quieter. As I climbed, water flowed down around my feet, on its way to the lake below. I hadn't taken into consideration the summer snow melt from the mountaintops. Everything was soggy, steep, overgrown, or a bear trail. Frustrated, I set up camp in a small, dry valley between two hills, near the lake, which was dicey at best. My tent was less than fifty feet away from an extremely busy bear pathway, but it was both dry and level. I was clearly at the mercy of the bears.

From my campsite, I could see bears in the distance. They scurried along the lake, so far away that they looked like weasels. To my surprise, not a single bear came by my tent the entire first afternoon or evening. I kept up my guard, but began to think that the Grizzly Maze might be one big relaxing vacation. Things changed radically the next morning.

Around six A.M. a bear woke me from sleep and nearly climbed into the tent. With almost human dexterity, the bear pulled the front tent flap aside and peered in at me. I screamed and scrambled for a can of bear mace. Undaunted, the bear sat down on its rump and swayed from side to side, trying to look in at me while I floundered about the tent, searching for the mace. I finally located the spray and had uncapped the can before I realized that this calm, curious bear meant no harm. Wild animals can be unpredictable, but as my head cleared and my heart slowed, I sensed only peaceful intentions from the bear.

Setting the mace aside, I quietly unzipped the front screen, clearly revealing the visitor. It was a young bear, about four or five years old, with a short brown coat and a ring of long frosted hair around its neck. I recognized the visitor: It was Melissa, a bear I'd met the previous season. Melissa's doglike snout and sparkling brown eyes looked at me in wonder.

"Oh, Melissa," I said softly. "You really gave me a start this morning. You're the very first bear to greet me out here in the Grizzly Maze. Lucky me. You're such a sweet, beautiful bear." Melissa rolled onto her back, scratching and squirming contentedly. She lay still for several minutes, then rolled to all fours. "Thank you for your visit," I said. She blinked several times, then turned and slowly shuffled off.

I was almost back to sleep when another female paid a visit to my tent. Her name was Kate, and she was just as friendly and inquisitive as Melissa, pressing her nose against the mesh to see what was inside. I couldn't decide if I thought Kate was a beautiful or a homely bear. She certainly looked different. Her body was pear-shaped, and her coat was naturally shaved, just like Melissa's. In fact, she had a similar tuft of frosted blond hair that jutted out around her neck. I was fairly sure that Kate and Melissa were sisters. Kate's head and neck were most peculiar—the neck extended like a hose, and the head was shaped more like a dog's than a brown grizzly bear's. Kate and Melissa had just entered the beginning of their breeding years. I had found each to be kind and responsible bears, perfect for grizzly motherhood. Kate checked me out for a bit, then moved on.

I was interrupted a third time by a young male named Buster. Buster was only four or five years old, but he was obviously successful at catching fish. His golden-brown fur stretched like an overblown balloon around his stout body. He had a very easygoing disposition, which suited me just fine. If all went well for Buster, he could become a huge grizzly. Years from now I wanted to be on Buster's good side, for it would make my studies much safer.

Buster seemed nervous about passing the tent, and stopped in front, fidgeting, so I spoke to him. Buster perked up, swept in for a closer look, then cheerfully moved along. The three successive visits told me that this was going to be a busy location.

At eleven A.M. I packed my extensive camera gear, threw in a Power Bar and a quart of Tang, and headed for the bear tunnels. First, I had to wade around the lake through waist-deep water. At times the water reached my shoulders, forcing me to carry my gear head high. The most difficult part of trudging through the lake was keeping my balance on the slick rocks that covered the bottom. A misstep would destroy my valuable camera equipment, and I nearly slipped a dozen times. Finally, I made my way across the lake and on to the real challenge of the tunnels.

Although there were countless routes, there was one tunnel that was wider and clearer than the rest. I decided that the wider path looked like the main tunnel. My best guess was that the tunnel was at least a quarter of a mile long, and I trembled at the entrance. Just as I was about to step in, a massive set of paw prints caught my eye. I used a pocket tape measurer to check the diameter and length. The front measured ten inches wide, while the back was an astonishing seventeen inches long. My heart nearly stopped. Somewhere close, at least one prehistoric-sized bear roamed the

Grizzly Maze. I hunched forward and stepped inside.

The daylight disappeared under the canopy of branches. As my eyes slowly adjusted, I found that I could see a very short distance ahead. The tunnel was about four feet high and five feet wide, though its size varied as I moved along. The shaft cut through a thick gray tangle of alders, but branches reached out, tearing at my face and body. I listened intently: On the narrow path, a bear coming from the opposite direction would collide with me. I had never been so scared.

Suddenly, I heard the telltale sound of crashing bushes and thudding steps, then loud huffing puffs of breath. A bear was approaching and I needed to do something fast. Staying on the trail was out of the question, and turning to run was foolish. I wriggled and shimmied into the wall of alders. Then I sat down, low and silent, close to the tunnel. A large male rumbled by, stopping to sniff my footprints. He wasn't the mammoth grizzly who'd made the paw prints outside the tunnel, but he was big, at least 800 pounds. As he turned and looked at me, I silently cursed myself for entering the tunnels. Then, inexplicably, he turned and vanished through the trees. Now I was trapped in the Maze. I no longer wanted to head out, because I was afraid that I would run into the big grizzly. I had no choice but to reenter the trail and continue on, bracing myself for anything.

Within seconds another bear approached. Again, I hastily stepped into the brush and waited. Blood trickled down my face, from cuts I'd gotten from the branches. This time, the bear that appeared was familiar to me. It was Kate, one of the young females that had visited my tent earlier in the day. She froze, ears laid back, clearly agitated. Undoubtedly, traveling the tunnels can be unsettling for bears, too, especially young ones like Kate. "Hiya, Kate," I called out gently. "It sure is scary in here, isn't it, girl?" Kate relaxed at the sound of my voice. As she stretched toward me her ears perked up, and all signs of stress melted away. "I wish you could tell me how much farther it is to the salmon creek," I said to the young bear. Kate looked at me, then disappeared through the tunnel. Eager to be out of the Maze's tunnels, I quickly moved on.

Finally, I heard the unmistakable sound of running water. As I got closer to the sound of the creek, the tunnel splintered off into many branches. Which way to go? Would one lead me to a waiting grizzly? There was no way to tell. I picked one, hoping for the best. The trail I chose rose steeply and steadily. At last I broke through, twenty feet above the creek, to the most incredible sight of my life.

They were everywhere! The entire creek was crammed with bears. Directly below me fished a giant bulging brown, a thousand, maybe thirteen hundred pounds. Downstream, at least ten more were working. On my right, a dozen bears walked through the rocky creek. On the opposite side of a hill bordering the creek, two mother bears crawled along, each with spring cubs. Along the bank, twenty feet from me, numerous others were eating salmon. The creek bed was littered with the remains of salmon. Fish guts, skin, and bones were everywhere.

I hid behind the thick green grass and saucer-sized flowers, overlooking the feast. I had stumbled upon an amazing grizzly gathering, the likes of which may never have been seen before by humans. Abruptly, my camouflaged perch was invaded by a sizable bear, anxious to push through and fish. At first the bear ignored me, but in its haste nearly bowled me over the side, right into the throng of salmon-frenzied bears!

Then the bear began to exhibit stress. I was trapped on the cliff, and had to respond. Years of studying bears had taught me that during major salmon runs, brown grizzlies were more tolerant of other life because of the abundance of food. I needed to relax and become as much like a bear as possible.

I leaned back, slowly snapping my mouth and huffing slightly from my throat. I looked down, avoiding the gaze of the nearby bear. He pushed by, his salmon-swollen belly rubbing along my left knee. Another large bear dropped in from above and behind, jamming foliage into my back. I could smell their sweet, furry bodies and salmon-scented breath as they crisscrossed paths. Without a doubt they knew I was there, but they ignored my presence. I was beginning to feel like a real grizzly.

For about an hour I took pictures from my spot above the creek. Directly below, the massive grizzly allowed me an intimate glimpse of his feeding session. At times he tossed huge slabs of rock, some at least five hundred pounds, aside to uncover hidden fish. As the rocks crashed on the creek bed, the vibrations shook me. There was so much fish available that the giant began to eat only the fattiest parts of the salmon. He skinned the fish, ate the head, and sloppily squeezed the roe of the decapitated salmon into his mouth. After an hour the giant was finally sated and left the creek. As he splashed and crashed across, most of the other animals scrambled out of his path. It was time for me to make a move and cross the creek.

There were only six grizzlies in the creek as I crawled to the opposite side, trying to behave as much like a bear as possible despite my camera equipment. I crossed as if on all fours, holding my tripod and waterproof bag over my head and using my free hand as a paw. The bears paid no attention to me. Scrambling up the opposite bank, I set up my cameras and tripod and photographed the action. Some of the bears were so close, I had to use less than a 100-millimeter lens to get their bodies into the frame. I even used a wide 20-millimeter lens as one animal passed under my nose without concern. Certainly the bears of the remote Maze had never seen a human on their fishing grounds, yet they clearly tolerated me. The combination of their salmon frenzy and lack of previous human contact made my presence possible.

Among the discarded salmon carcasses were living fish attempting to lay fertilized eggs, the miracle of spawning. The bears of the Grizzly Maze ate a species of salmon known as sockeye, or red salmon. Later in the season, three other species of salmon would spawn in the waters of the Maze, and even in the Grizzly Sanctuary: chum, silver, and pink salmon. A fifth species, king salmon, inhabited Alaskan waters, but it did not journey to the Maze or the Grizzly Sanctuary.

Salmon are born and die in the same river. Once they have reached their ancestral spawning grounds, the fully mature fish seek beds of gravel, from which the females excavate the spawning grounds, or redds, sometimes to a depth of fifty centimeters, or nearly 20 inches.[11] Females then shed their eggs, or roe, while the males provide the fertilizing milt, which is fish sperm.

Fertilized eggs develop slowly during the winter and hatch toward spring. The small emerging salmon, or alevin, retains a large mass of yolk from the egg to feed on. After the yolk is absorbed and depleted, the salmon is called fry, and feeds on insects and small aquatic animals for several weeks.

The fry that grow become fingerlings, and remain in the home waters for a year or longer. After reaching maturity (the smolt stage), the journey to the sea begins. Salmon remain at sea from two to five years, depending on the species. The sockeye tend to stay out about two years, king salmon average five.

Salmon are a keystone species in an ecosystem. The very survival of many animals is directly attributed to the success of salmon. Besides natural difficulties, salmon must survive myriad problems caused by man, like long fishing lines, gill nets, seines, and sport fishing. In addition, careless forestry, pollution, and power dams have devastated populations of salmon worldwide.

Brown grizzly bears can easily eat over 100 pounds of salmon in a day. While I watched from across the creek, the bears of the Grizzly Maze were eating at least that much. Fishing techniques varied, ranging from snatch and grab to complete submersion and scavenging under rocks.

Kate returned through one of the tunnels and began fishing

alongside Melissa. They joined an old male, Quincy, who I had observed in my two previous expeditions to the Maze. Quincy had a shaggy faded brown coat, and trusting dark droopy eyes, like a raggedy old stuffed toy come to life. His mouth hung open, red tongue protruding. Quincy appeared to be over twenty years old, but he still seemed strong. With magnificent fish runs such as these, Quincy may well have a few years left in him. I hoped to see Quincy for seasons to come.

A round, frosted-blond bear gradually worked its way next to me on the banks of the creek. When the bear turned its back, I couldn't help but notice that this was a female. She was one of the prettiest bears I'd ever seen, and I named her Snowball. As I photographed her at close range with a Minolta 80–200 millimeter APO2.8 lens, she gave me full-frame demonstrations on how to dissect and eat salmon.

From the corner of my eye, I saw a dark male enter the creek and spook some of the other bears. He wasn't gigantic as adult males go, only about 800 pounds. His dark, sleek coat shimmered in the creek, and his grizzly face was sharp and pointed at the snout. But his eyes were manic and wary, sending a chill up my spine: I'd seen those eyes before. This was Demon, what some experts label the "25th Grizzly," one that tolerates no man or bear, one that will kill without bias. Almost a year ago to the day, I had thought that Demon was going to kill me in the Grizzly Maze.

I had been walking in the open, along the shoreline of the lake during my second visit to the Maze. The day was simply perfect, warm and cloudless, with just enough of a breeze to ground the flying insects. As I walked toward the outlet of the front creek carrying my camera equipment, I noticed a shiny black adult male strutting in my direction. Not concerned, I reached the creek and decided to cross to give the dark male the right of way up the creek. After crossing, I had set up the camera a distance away, hoping to get a picture of the grizzly. The black grizzly ignored the path along the creek, and, instead, crossed the water toward me. Slightly puzzled, I folded up my gear and backed away. My guess was that he'd hit the bank on my side, make a sharp left, and continue on to the fishing grounds. But as I backed up, he did not turn away. I simply worked my way up a steep, grassy hill so that the dark male would have plenty of room, and access to all the paths. However, when the black bear continued toward me, I became very concerned. I tried to decipher his body language, but I couldn't see any outwardly aggressive signals. His ears were up and his back hair was calm. He didn't woof, huff, or chomp; he wasn't grinding his teeth, popping his jaw, or foaming at the mouth. In fact, he seemed rather nonchalant. But the dark male edged slowly up, making my retreat up the hill futile. Dumbfounded, I held my ground without speaking. Just as the dark male closed to within ten feet, his ears went back, and the most menacing, wicked eyes I'd ever seen turned to ice. The dark male was coming for me. In a last desperate moment, I lunged toward him, kicking and screaming. Confused, the dark male retreated slightly. I continued charging and growling, and he slowly backed off, those wicked eyes blinking. There's a lot of bluff and huff in the world of grizzly encounters, but I wasn't bluffing: I was obviously ready to die fighting. I hadn't thought the black male was bluffing either, but at that point, he hadn't felt like working up a sweat killing me.

Later that same evening, while I had tried to sleep, I heard heavy grizzly steps and huffs just outside my tent. The August night sky was clear, with a brilliant full moon that lit up the Grizzly Maze. An animal's muzzle poked at the flimsy mesh of the back window of the tent, blowing powerful puffs of air into my face. I could see those same maniacal eyes, glowing with the reflection of the full moon. I jumped out of my tent with a flashlight and a can of Counter Assault bear mace.

"Leave me alone, Demon!" I yelled. "I need some sleep!"

Demon moved to my left, hidden in some head-high weeds. I flicked on my heavy-duty waterproof high-beam flashlight, but got no more than a feeble ray of light barely brighter than a match. Demon's eyes flickered through the nearby tall grass. "Demon, get the hell out of here!" I shouted. "I'll be gone soon, and you can have the whole damn place! Just give me this night!"

I could hear Demon moving off ever so slowly. Then, only fifteen feet from me, I heard obvious sounds of digging. Demon was either excavating a bed or digging a hole for my corpse. "Demon, don't you even think about sleeping there!" I clapped my hands loudly and urged him to move on. But after some more digging, I heard a restful "Aahh" from the bear. "Come on, Demon, don't sleep there! How am I going to get any rest with your scary ass so close?" A few minutes later I heard loud snoring and gave up. The most frightening bear had decided to be my neighbor.

My wristwatch, which glowed brighter than that stupid flashlight, read 1:30 A.M. I retreated to the imagined safety of my tent and shuddered for two hours, until exhaustion overcame my fear. At seven-thirty A.M. I opened my eyes, happy to be alive. Creeping from the tent, I tiptoed through the high grass. There was Demon's big, black rump! He was still there, snoring away.

That was the last time I had seen Demon. Now, a year later, he was back, fishing in the creek. I shuddered, trying hard not to meet his gaze. Fortunately, he disappeared without incident, into the tunnels of the Maze.

Shortly after, a mother bear, Tobi, accompanied by her yearling Squiggle, made a fishing debut. I'd met them a year ago, just like Demon, but under better circumstances. Squiggle had been a shy, roly-poly six-month-old. I had watched Squiggle learn to fish on one of his very first trips to the front creek. Tobi's frenzied fishing techniques would knock Squiggle over and dump him below the surface. He would then thrust his back legs against the bottom and shoot up through the surface, gasping for air. For a minute, Tobi would stop and carefully reassure her cub, then she would resume the reckless fishing process all over again. A year later, Squiggle had grown in size and confidence. Both he and Tobi were eating liberally.

I took a fairly open position along the creek bank, watching the grizzly fishing spectacle. There was no way to tell exactly how many bears were in the area. Some bears snared fish and darted back through one of the dozens of tunnels along the creek. Others fished for a spell, then left, to be replaced by more bears. There were easily fifty different bears, and I was awed to be standing in their company.

Snowball waddled by and planted herself in the creek. Her stuffed belly made her look as wide as she was long. The abundance of fish meant she could eat only her favorite parts. I watched with fascination as she went through the process. First, she trapped a sockeye between her dexterous claws and slapped it against a boulder. Next, she stripped the silvery skin away and sucked it down her throat like spaghetti. A bite beheaded the salmon. Snowball seemed to relish the eyes and brains most. Then, with the bulk of the meat remaining, she released the fish downstream for other, less proficient bears to feed on. A flock of noisy seagulls hovered above Snowball, waiting for exactly the right moment to snatch a bite.

After losing all track of time, my own sensations demanded I head back to my camp for a human-style lunch. I hesitantly approached the tunnels. They were the only way back, so I plunged through. I didn't meet any bears along the way, and that was just fine by me.

Leaving the tunnels, I saw two subadults play-fighting in the lake, splashing and thrashing. With the abundance of food that the salmon runs provided, the bears had extra free time and energy to play. I found two more adolescents playfully duking it out near my tent. They fought within fifty feet of it, and couldn't have cared less about me. I photographed a few rounds, then went in for a nap while they tore up the neighborhood.

A moderate rain fell for the next forty-eight hours, pinning me inside and forcing the bears to bed down. I rested, relaxed, and updated my diary. When the sunshine returned, so did the bears. They began strolling through my camp like people on a Sunday walk in a city park. Snowball visited, along with a horde of nameless and faceless grizzlies, some passing so close they brushed the sides of the tent. They were all so well fed they could spend time leisurely studying me! Snowball was particularly interested in my routine activities. She sat and watched as I strapped on my shoes. The two playful male subadults reappeared, frolicked some more, then fell asleep a mere twenty feet away. I had to walk around them to go to the lake and bathe. While scrubbing, a mother with two yearlings wandered by. I greeted them with a cheerful "Good morning!" A small subadult shot from the grassy valley and ran directly toward me on the stone-covered beach. The grizzly was so little I called him Peanut. He was probably just 2½ years old, and had recently been sent out on his own. At first, he was startled by my presence, but settled down when I sang to him. He must have enjoyed my song, because he advanced toward me. There was nowhere to go but back into the lake, so I held my ground. I could have run him off but it just didn't feel right. Peanut tilted his muzzle and poked it at my outstretched fingers, delicately licking them. I returned the favor, leaning forward to kiss him on his damp nose. Peanut held my gaze for a moment, then turned and walked on to what I hoped would be a happy, prosperous life.

After the encounter with Peanut, it was time to take advantage of the fine weather and return to the back creek. However, there was a slight problem with my plan: The entire small valley around my tent had filled with bears. There were two different subadult gangs, each with about four members. A mother with two spring cubs hid a short distance from the tent. Several other bears either loitered on or passed through the main path of the valley itself. The thought of leaving the tent unattended made me extremely nervous, so I decided to wait a few hours. Eventually, the activity calmed down to a dull roar, and I decided to chance it. Luck was on my side, and I passed through the tunnels without incident.

At the creek, things had slowed. The massive salmon run was over, at least for the time being. Once again, I crossed the creek on all fours. The few bears that were around ignored me. Then Demon came out of one of the tunnels and immediately zeroed in on me. As soon as I reached the opposite side of the creek, Demon began to stalk me. Today, there was no salmon to distract him. I tried to scoop up all of my cameras and retreat into one of the tunnels, but I was so unnerved that I dropped my equipment, then realized that I either had to leave it or stand my ground. Today, all of the fight was drained out of me. I couldn't gather up all of my gear quickly enough, so with no place to go, I surrendered. I just hoped that it wouldn't hurt too much.

Demon crossed the creek menacingly, ears laid back, ready to pounce. As Demon advanced, I looked into his frightening eyes and chanted, "I love you, Demon, please kill me quickly!" over and over. Demon stopped. He stepped back into the creek and effortlessly flipped a quarter-ton boulder aside, revealing some trapped salmon. He speared an exposed fish, and aggressively bit its head off. His forty-two teeth dripped with blood. "Nice set of teeth, Demon," I complimented the bear. He was still frightening, but the threat had ebbed. Demon turned to other massive slabs, tossing them aside like small stones. Demon was a majestic animal in the prime of his life, with the power to decapitate me in an instant. His warning was clear: "We may be beautiful, but we're always capable of killing." That message must be accepted by anyone who chooses to walk among the grizzlies.

Great opportunities can come out of some of the worst circumstances. During the encounter with Demon I had instinctively backed up a short distance, toward the opening of the tunnels. After Demon settled down, it occurred to me that it might be a good idea to make myself scarce. Going back to my tent was impossible as long as Demon worked the creek, since trying to cross it with him around would be playing Russian roulette. Traveling in the tunnels was something that I had wanted to keep to a minimum, yet there was something intriguing about this tunnel, which called to the reckless adventurer in me. As I kicked the thought around, Demon glanced over with a menacing look. I scrambled into and up the tunnel in a flash.

The tunnel ran up a steep hill bordering the creek. It was roomier inside than the thin, long tunnel that connected the two salmon creeks. It was at least ten feet wide, and arched well over my head. The floor was fine-grained sand, worn down from centuries of use. On closer inspection it became clear to me that the bears literally slid down the tunnel, leaving long stretches of plowed sand. Instantly I imagined being crushed by a grizzly sliding down the shaft. However, it was much too exciting in the tunnel to give up. I continued to climb, straining to hear a descending bear.

Other tunnels and paths branched off my route. It became surreal and confusing. The entangled alder branches overhead concealed the sky. The potent, sweet whiffs of bear odor were intoxicating. Fresh, old, and ancient scat littered the tunnel. Finally, after climbing hundreds of feet, I saw a brilliant light from a distant opening. Suddenly, the beam of light was blocked out. A massive bear had entered the shaft.

The huge grizzly sat down on its bottom, rocking oddly back and forth. Then it began to slide down toward me. I tried to push through the alder walls, but they were too dense. The bear closed in, growling! I slid down wildly, trying to escape the bear. My bottom began heating up from the friction of my slide. Still, the giant bear gained on me, closing the distance between us. I passed the entrance to one of the many connecting paths, then quickly braked at the next and propelled myself into it. The giant bear whooshed by without seeing me.

Sand oozed from my clothing and ears. I hastily checked inside my Tamrac photo backpack. Grains of sand can be as destructive to camera equipment as water. Everything inside was safe. Another piece of donated gear had saved the expedition.

Still shaking, I reentered the main tunnel and headed up toward the light. At last I made it to the top. I gasped at the view: a narrow, sandy path clinging to an imposing mountain. Below its sheer edge, the waters of the salmon creek danced furiously. In the distance, a magnificent blue-green lake lay shimmering, a series of waterfalls cascading around the perimeter. The tunnel I climbed through was part of a passage that led out of the Maze and into the endless wilderness.

I walked warily along the foot path. It was surprisingly level, and frighteningly narrow. It was obvious what the bears did when they crossed paths. In the past, I had seen bears climb steep mountains as if they were spiders. For animals like the grizzlies, the path was a convenient route, but they could step off at any time, and safely climb the mountain. For me, stepping from the path meant certain death. The exposed outdoor path led to more tunnels burrowed into the mountain. Deciding that I had gone far enough along the path, I took a tunnel up a bit higher, hoping to get an even better view.

The tunnel I chose constricted with each step. Protruding branches poked at my face and tore off my glasses. Exposed roots and jagged rocks had replaced the soft, sandy floor. The tunnel became congested with shrubbery, and eventually petered out. It was time to give up, but I wanted that big view. I pushed up through the brush, huffing like an angry bear. Sweat poured from my body, and I slipped and fell, ripping a gash in my water-resistant hiking pants. The Maze's jungle of alders had closed in on me. I was lost.

The quickest solution would have been to head back down. The high ground I had reached held little interest for the bears, so the tunnels had disappeared. Finally, I broke through a curtain of alder and into the open terrain. But my "big view" was eclipsed by still higher mountains. Basically, I couldn't see much more than I had from the path below. The only difference up here was that everything was smaller. Being stubborn didn't always pay off.

Or did it? In the clearing on the mountain there was a peculiar excavation. I carefully climbed across the sharply angled landscape and realized that I had made a major personal discovery—I had found a bear's winter den.

It made sense. I was easily above 1,000 feet in elevation, and the dig site faced the direction that precipitation was most likely to come from. Bear dens on Kodiak Island averaged about 1,800 feet in elevation, while dens of western coastal Alaska averaged 1,300 feet.[12]

The den appeared to have been dug by a large bear. I made some measurements and found it to be larger than others I had read about. The entrance was forty-three inches wide, and opened into a tunnel of similar dimensions that angled down sharply. Inch by inch, I crawled through nervously, holding a butane light for illumination. The yard-long tunnel emptied into an amazing chamber that was lined with a small amount of old, dried foliage. The sleeping chamber was longer than I am, at least seven feet, and was five feet wide. I tried to stand up in the chamber, but jammed my head into the ceiling. Dazed, I fell to the soft floor. I chuckled at my stupidity, then curled up, like a hibernating bear. I imagined it to be below freezing outside, with a raging snowstorm. Inside the den of the great bear I was invincible, safe from the deadly elements.

Typically, the bear that used the den would have entered in November, although depending on the conditions, bears can enter their dens any time from October through December. Male bears tend to leave first, in late March or April. Mother bears with that year's cubs tend to stay in the den longer, leaving between late April and early June.

During a bear's sleep, the heart rate slows from a normal 98 beats per minute to only 8 to 10 beats per minute. The body temperature only falls a few degrees from the normal 99 degrees.[13] If the bear's core temperature falls below 89 degrees, it will automatically awaken. During hibernation, a bear typically loses 15 to 30 percent of its body weight as fat breaks down, providing the body with food and water. On average, 3,000 to 4,000 calories are expended each day, discharged through body heat. Some bears, especially mothers nursing cubs, wake up emaciated, while others emerge in excellent shape. It was doubtful that I would ever completely understand the dynamics of hibernation, but for the brief time that I napped in the chamber, I could almost feel it.

I reluctantly left the den to head back down the mountain. I was not only sad to leave the winter home behind, but also dreading the descent ahead.

I summoned up my courage, and tentatively entered the chute. Slowly I inched forward, careful not to lose control on the steep incline. I kept a wary ear tuned to bear traffic behind me. Finally, I reached the end of the tunnels, and cautiously looked around for entering grizzlies. The coast was clear, so I hurried on to the creek.

Fish were no longer spawning at the creek, but had begun to gather at the outlet in the lake. A pair of large males were catching salmon in the outlet. I crawled through a connecting tunnel that emptied at the spot where the creek spilled into the clear lake. One of the males was Freckles. I called him Freckles because the curly hairs on his wet face looked like polka dots. Freckles had an extraordinary fishing technique.

He deep-sea dove, paddling underneath the lake's surface in search of salmon. I had seen this technique used by other bears, notably a world-famous bear named Diver who lived at Katmai

National Park's Brooks River. Diver also plunged underwater for extended periods in search of fish. But in all honesty, I thought that Freckles could outdo Diver. First, Freckles paddled thirty feet out into the lake and then submerged himself. I timed Freckles, and on average, he stayed under for about a minute. Many times, he would come up a hundred feet from where he dove in. When successful, he would paddle back to shore clutching a fish. Freckles often ate the fish twenty feet from me without a care. During his dives, I could usually keep track of his underwater progress by tracking the bursts of bubbles that crackled and blew to the surface. Once, after a dive went on for more than two minutes, I began to panic. It was years since I had lifeguarded, but on that day, I thought I might have to come out of retirement. I instantly imagined myself diving into the lake toward a half ton of lifeless brown bear. I'd reach out with my left hand, grasping Freckles's blunt left claw, and pull up toward the surface. Then, as Freckles's body rotated on to its back, I'd attempt my lifeguard cross-chest carry and pull the bear from the water. There was no way I could wrap my arm around his massive chest, so I'd have to opt for the second strategy of a double chin pull while kicking hard underneath. Getting his fat butt out of the water would also be a real problem. Hopefully, one of the onlookers like Snowball, or maybe Demon, would lend a paw. Then, I'd perform mouth-to-snout resuscitation while the curious grizzlies watched. Finally, Freckles would gurgle and cough back to life. For good measure, I'd wrap my shirts and jacket around his drenched furry body to warm him up. Last but not least, I'd advise him on the dangers of staying underwater too long, and would recommend the use of a flotation device or a diving-buddy bear system. Just as this wild fantasy was about to become a reality, Freckles exploded from the deep with a mouthful of salmon. Well, I'd keep an eye on him for a while longer, just in case.

Relieved that Freckles was safe, I went back to my camp.

Would there be anything left? Entering the clearing, I smiled as I saw my home-sweet-tent perfectly intact. Thank God! There were still a lot of bears around, but for whatever reason, they had decided not to destroy my home.

The next morning I saw a mother with a spring cub drinking from the lake, just below me. The cub was feeble, scrawny, and dragging its hind quarters in pain. The cub was pulling itself around in a desperate effort to keep up with its mother. The mother displayed no outward compassion for her struggling cub: It would have to persevere or perish. I wanted to rescue the cub and nurse it back to health in a more caring environment, but I knew that couldn't be. Back in the Grizzly Sanctuary I had aided Mickey, but there was no way I could come between a mother and her cub. This time I was just going to have to follow the rules of nature, terrible as they might be.

The pair passed by my tent, which frightened the mother. She was either going to flee or charge. I sang them a song, trying to calm her down. She sat and listened while the cub pricked up its ears. Then they both relaxed and enjoyed the entertainment. "God," I prayed as they moved along, "I may not be worth much, but please take special care of this cub."

Instead of taking her handicapped cub through the dangerous tunnels, the mother bear swam with the cub across the lake. This route was not only safer, but swimming was therapeutic for the cub. Perhaps there was hope for the baby after all.

After I watched the pair cross the water, I turned my attention to the fishing bears. I crawled on all fours to the bank of the creek and set up my camera, hoping that the bears would not concern themselves with me.

A young adult bear named Taffy was the most active. At about six or seven, Taffy was chubby, with gorgeous chocolate fur. His handsome face had a comical air because one ear drooped. The droopy ear was probably the result of a play fight with his wrestling partner, Quick. Taffy and Quick loved to spar, and play-fought several times a day while I was in the Maze.

Taffy's fishing technique was part diver, part acrobat. He stood at the edge of the creek, contemplating his plunge for as long as fifteen minutes. When the right moment finally came, he leaped into the water with his head up and claws pointed. He landed in the water with a tremendous plop. Taffy didn't always come up with a fish, but, nonetheless, he seemed to enjoy every dive. A third of the time Taffy caught a fish, paddled it back to the creek bank, and devoured it. Sometimes when Taffy missed, he would swim over next to me, blowing bubbles and blinking. I'd encourage him to get back out there. "Go get 'em, Taffy! Show those fish who's boss!" Taffy always plunged back in.

Much to my delight, Snowball seemed to be going through a late estrous period, and Taffy was courting her. It was probably her second estrous cycle, though occasionally female bears did not come into estrous until late July. The duration of estrous is quite variable, just like everything else in bears. Research had told me that a bear's period of estrous is seven to ten days. However, my own studies were showing exceptions to this rule.[14] I saw Taffy pursuing Snowball around the lake, sniffing repeatedly at her rump. Later, Snowball joined Taffy and copied his fishing technique. Snowball crashed into the lake with a dramatic dive, her golden-blond fur disappearing under the surface. Once, she came up with a fish so tiny I thought it was a fry. Snowball clutched it, beaming with success, and ate it out in the lake as if it were the biggest and most delicious fish in the entire world. Snowball also swam over and visited with me. "Are you going to have Taffy's babies?" I asked. "They're going to be the silliest cubs in the whole world!" I told her.

During the best fishing runs, the large males dominated, but when the fish were sparse in the main part of the creek, subordinate bears took over. I liked these lulls, because it was pleasant to see the smaller younger bears and mothers with cubs get a fair shake. As Taffy, Snowball, and Freckles fished the outlet, other bears sneaked in from behind. While hidden by some thick bushes, I saw Peanut working industriously in the creek. Peanut lifted small rocks, looking for scraps of trapped salmon. Some of the boulders were just too heavy for him to lift, but Peanut still tried, huffing and puffing with effort. Peanut was nervous and kept a constant watch for the larger or higher-ranking bears that could displace him. Unfortunately for Peanut, that was virtually every other bear in the Grizzly Maze. Peanut detected my movement, and became extremely frightened. I quickly stepped out and identified myself; he settled down immediately, going back to excavating rocks and scavenging bits of dead fish.

Meanwhile, back at the outlet, Taffy pulled out all the stops and began putting on a real show, hurling himself into the lake. He didn't eat much of what he caught; for the most part he was just cooling off on the warm, cloudless day. A small crowd of bears gathered to watch, attracted by the loud splashing belly flops. Freckles, Snowball, and Taffy's wrestling partner, Quick, stared hypnotically, their heads bobbing with each leap and thunderous splash. Eventually Quick, a grayish grizzly similar in size to Taffy, joined in. After Quick's second plunge, Taffy ambushed him from behind and they began a playful brawl. The pair embraced in a true bear hug while wading through the lake. They slapped and nipped with reckless abandon and waltzed directly in front of me. Taffy turned from Quick's grip and reached for my body with an outstretched claw. I backed up, flattered but alarmed. Wrestling with a pair of seven-hundred-pound imps would be lethal for a wimp like me. "What's the big idea?!" I called to Taffy. "Three's a crowd, you goofball!" Taffy looked down at me, then went back to playing with Quick.

With the males sidetracked, Snowball took advantage of the salmon-pool opening. She worked up a head of steam and crashed loudly into the water from the creek bank. Again she came to the surface with another miniature fish in her incisors. As she ate, Freckles went out into the deep water. Not to be left out, I put aside my cameras and dove into the lake. I swam, connected to the bears by the same waters they enjoyed. It was summer in the grizzly wilderness, and we were the cleanest, happiest animals in Alaska. After the dip in the lake, the bears left and napped along the shore. Taffy and Snowball slept together, snoring gently. I hadn't seen a more congenial brown bear than Taffy since my days with Beacon in the Grizzly Sanctuary. Taffy was gregarious, bouncing between his male friends Freckles and Quick and his girlfriend Snowball. Somewhere in between, he even shared some time with me. Since not too much was happening, I, too, fell asleep, waking only after Taffy hurtled back into the lake.

Most bears traveled back and forth through the tunnels between the front and back creek several times a day. Taffy spent most of his time at the back creek with the diving platform, but he did make the trip through the tunnels to the front creek several times a day. Traveling through the tunnels was an extremely intimidating experience for me until I had a revelation: With the right timing, I could enter the tunnel behind Taffy and safely be escorted through. Taffy was dominant over most of the bears in the Maze, and so I was able to go in right behind him and breeze through the tunnels.

How was I able to establish this kind of intimate connection with the wild brown grizzlies? Bear history helps to explain. The earliest carnivores, Miacids evolved over 55 million years ago. The *Miacidae* family is extinct, but it gave rise to two super families: *Canoidea* (dogs, bears, weasels, and raccoons), and *Feloidea* (cats, hyenas, civets, and mongooses). Within the *Canoidea* family, the *Hemicyon*, or half dog, appears to be the lineage leading to bears. The *Hemicyon* displayed physical characteristics of both bears and dogs, and indicate the related evolutionary descent of wolves, weasels, and bears. Most, if not all, bear biologists will tell you that the bear's closest living relative is the dog. My interactions and studies have certainly shown similarities between bears' behavior and dogs': Booble follows me, Lazy sleeps at the tent, and Peanut licks my fingers. Possibly, the same primal aspects that bond dogs to humans may draw the grizzlies to me.

There are other clues to my acceptance by bears in the habitat and social conditions of the bears I live among. These animals are coastal brown bears, historically more tolerant than other types of bears. These bears migrate in large numbers to areas with abundant food sources. Competition between grizzlies for food in a finite area forces the bears to develop their social skills. A recognized social hierarchy and tolerance among the grizzlies reduces the levels of aggression to a minimum. These bears live in remote, fairly inaccessible habitats that are legally off limits to human hunters. Consequently, humans have contributed only slight adverse pressures, mostly by way of illegal poaching.

The final factor in the equation is myself. I live among the bears as one of them with virtually zero ecological impact. My strategy is one of complete immersion within the hierarchy of bears that is both respectful and peaceful. It would be quite interesting to know what the bears think I am; whether they consider me just another bear, an animal like Timmy the Fox, or something altogether different. Whatever their evaluation, it is abundantly clear that most of the bears I live among either tolerate me, or enjoy my company.

The rewards of my solitary, low impact technique will help the animals and people alike. For the animals, my presence offers a shield of protection from human displacement and poaching. For people, my studies will help in understanding the natural ways of the bears and will make a contribution toward their preservation.

Overnight, a storm arrived. In the morning, I reluctantly stepped from the tent to relieve myself. Heading back, a lump of soppy fur under some adjacent alders caught my eye. One part of the rain-soaked hide was blondish, and the other quite dark, with a telltale bent floppy ear. Taffy and Snowball momentarily opened their eyes. "You sleep tight, children. I love you," I whispered. Then I climbed back into the tent, straining to hear their peaceful breath. I, too, went back to sleep, contented by the sense of having a family.

My several-week visit to the Maze was coming to an end. Soon a boat would arrive and take me to another major area to study. Already, the thought of leaving the Maze hurt. Just as in the Grizzly Sanctuary, I had grown deeply attached to these bears. But I needed to move on to a new area of the coast to observe different feeding patterns. The best way to help bears is to study, document, and protect these gatherings of grizzlies so that I can successfully campaign for their preservation.

The rain did not stop me from saying good-bye to the bears. I went to the front creek and found Melissa, Kate, and Buster. They stood like statues in the pouring rain, waiting for fish. They straddled shallow waterfalls, staring as if they could will fish to materialize. I stood on the rocky shoreline and thanked them for their help, and wished them success in what remained of the feeding season. Next, I found Tobi and Squiggle just up the creek. If all went well, I hoped to find Squiggle here next season. Freckles popped out of one of the tunnels, scaring Tobi and Squiggle into early retirement for the day. It also gave me a chance to tell Freckles that thousands of humans would have a chance to learn about bear fishing thanks to his cooperation. I couldn't find Demon, and didn't really want to, but I still thanked him for sparing my life. I didn't see Peanut either, but I prayed for his successful survival, hoping to see him alive and well next year. It was easy to find Taffy and Snowball. They remained huddled snugly among the alder bushes near my tent. They picked up their heads at the sound of my approach.

"Easy, kids, it's just me," I reassured them. "I want you to have a lot of fun, make beautiful babies, and catch lots of fish to make your winter sleep easy. Please don't leave the safety of the Maze because there are men out there who will shoot you for trophies. If only people knew how wonderful you are. I'm sure then that they wouldn't want to hurt you. I'll try my best to teach them." I turned and left. I felt such love for these bears, for all bears. How could any person hurt them?

11

A boat came by that afternoon to pick me up. I was surprised that the boat made it on schedule. Rex, the captain of the twenty-eight-foot metal cruiser, pulled into a wind-protected bay and anchored. Then, aboard a motorized skiff, he came as close as possible to the valley and my campsite. He jumped out and greeted me warmly. Rex was tall and well built, deeply tanned, with even white teeth and a confident manner. Even on one of the worst days of the Alaska summer, Rex was upbeat.

"How ya doing, bear man?" Rex said.

"Just fine, Rex," I said. "You know, I wouldn't have been the least bit put off if you'd decided to postpone the charter on account of the weather."

"Nothing doing, Timothy. My cruiser thrives in the wet weather. It's a boat." He chuckled.

I put my stuff in the skiff and rode with Rex to the cruiser. The storm winds had picked up, and were blowing gale force. The waves were fifteen feet and building. I was sure that the danger of sinking was far greater than that of being harmed by a grizzly. I wanted to be safely back with Taffy and Snowball or in the Grizzly Sanctuary near Holly and Thumper. Trying to get my mind off the danger at hand, I went below and thought about my upcoming visit to the Forbidden Zone.

My first trip had taken place in early August 1994. I had sailed in on a cheap version of an inflatable Zodiac boat with a broken wooden floor and several slow leaks in each of its inflatable compartments. Every hour or two I had to stop and add air to the "S.S. Blowup Doll" with a foot pump.

The Forbidden Zone is located in a secluded bay along the far-western Pacific Ocean. A muddy, shallow shelf extends into the water a mile or so and denies access to nearly all boats and float planes. The actual shoreline is composed of soft, deep mud that even Bob couldn't touch down on in his plane. The largest grizzlies in the world live in the Forbidden Zone.

The owners of the Blowup Doll didn't know that I was going to the Forbidden Zone. They probably wouldn't have cared, because they were planning to discard the Doll and replace her with a more seaworthy vessel. But the Blowup Doll could get within the protective shelf of the Zone without a problem. Once in the shallow mud, I pulled the outboard prop up and paddled softly, skidding off the mucky bottom. The tattered Blowup Doll was my only way out. If a bear vandalized the craft, I would be marooned. This meant that in order to keep an eye on the boat I had to camp on the shoreline, right in the main path of the bears. At first, I wasn't too concerned, but the bears of the Forbidden Zone would teach me otherwise.

The lessons began within a half hour of my initial visit. Dark, angry bears came by my camp, huffing and frothing. A few charged directly, then veered off. Up until this point in my life, I had only been run at by Cupcake back in the Grizzly Sanctuary. By nightfall of the first day in the Forbidden Zone, I had been charged by four different bears. Sleep was nearly impossible as grizzlies whooshed and stomped through my camp all night. By morning, I was a basket case.

I tried to sleep in the safety of midday. The weather was particularly warm, and even the bears took a break. Unfortunately, the tent was like an oven, making sleep nearly impossible. I tried to nap outside, but the bugs attacked any exposed area of my body.

But I was determined not to give up. During my first stay, I had named only three bears, Grumpy, Stormy, and Killer. Each of these bears caught my attention by charging me. Grumpy was older, a large, nasty-tempered male of 1,000 pounds. He set a record by running after me three times in a single day.

Playing dead can sometimes be an effective passive survival strategy against attacking bears, but should only be implemented if physical contact is imminent. In the Forbidden Zone, playing dead might result in being dead, so I adopted a more radical and aggressive strategy. Each time a bear charged, I countered by screaming and rushing right back. Finally, after three tortuous days, I gave up.

I left the Forbidden Zone, planning not to return. I had no right to be in a place where I obviously was not welcome. Then I gave it some serious thought. I believed that the Forbidden Zone held a wealth of information and could provide insight into the behavior of bears. Studying and photographing the bears of the Forbidden Zone might really help my life's work. Also, if the bears living there were being poached, they needed my help and protection. However, it was clear to me that it would take a new strategy to live peacefully with the bears of the Forbidden Zone.

This time, as Rex maneuvered the boat into a protected harbor, I wondered what would happen to me in the Forbidden Zone.

Guarded by tall snow-clad mountains, immense blue glaciers, and raging rivers, the Forbidden Zone remains untouched by humans. Although it has no name on modern geographical maps, the Yupik Eskimos called it the Forbidden Zone for its nearly inaccessible location and its vicious bears. These were no ordinary bears: Adult males averaged eight to eleven feet from nose to rump, and weighed eight hundred to twelve hundred pounds, though it is believed that some weigh more than fifteen hundred pounds.

The tide was so high that the bank of tall grasses was almost submerged. It had the look of the Florida Everglades, but instead of gators guarding the swamps, these waters had big grizzlies. As Rex helped me haul my gear to a selected campsite, three different dark bears investigated us. Two of them began to charge, but retreated at the prospect of taking on two strange beings. I tried to appear brave in front of Rex, but deep down I was thinking, "Darn it, these bears are going to kick my ass again!"

"Nice place! Too bad I can't stay!" Rex quipped sarcastically. "Especially after that lovely boat ride!" With that, he jumped aboard the skiff and motored away.

My plan was to dress in black from head to toe to look as much like the local bears as possible. I would roll in fresh bear beds to alter my human odor, and crawl on all fours in front of the bears. I would try to remain silent, communicating only with the bears' huffs, woofs, and posturing.

With some high pressure, good weather was finally coming. The temperature, according to my high/low thermometer, had bottomed out at twenty-seven degrees Fahrenheit. In the early morning everything had frozen, turning the dew around my tent into icy frosting. Inside the tent, the temperature was just thirty-one degrees Fahrenheit.

The daytime was different. By midday the temperature in the shade quickly shot up to seventy degrees, and the inside of my tent reached a hundred degrees. Somewhere between day and night, there was maybe one hour when I was comfortable.

Toward early evening, the bears began to gather in the bay. Chum salmon, or dog salmon, lured them to the waters. There were few places left on earth where bears openly fished in ocean bays, because nearly all of the bears' traditional fishing bays had long since been invaded by people. The areas that remained were extremely remote, or were legally off limits to hunters. The Forbidden Zone was both.

I gathered up my photo gear and headed for the bay, crawling on all fours. The area where the bears gathered was at least a mile away, but I had no choice because the bears lurked in every direction. On the way to the fishing bay, I rolled in several bear beds, hoping to mask my scent.

I had planned to try and observe from a camouflaged area. However, since I was in an open bay, that strategy was impossible, because in open bay fishing, unlike the classic river fishing I had witnessed before, the bears would be incredibly spread out. I hoped that as long as I was dressed in black and on all fours, my chances of passing for a bear—at least from a distance—increased.

I crawled across the flat land. High grasses, spongy marshes, and tide-swollen streams coursed through the landscape. On all fours, I couldn't see over the grasses and a few alder shrubs. It took well over an hour for me to reach the fishing bay. So far, my strategy seemed to be working: The bears either ignored me, or didn't know I was there. Once I crawled out to the open bay, the true test would begin.

On hands and knees I crawled to the shoreline of the bay and began to observe. Approximately twenty-five bears were in the bay, scattered throughout the water. Some stood on shallow sandbars, while others were up to their necks in the water. It was very different from the intense activity of the crowded Grizzly Maze.

The fishing techniques were more violent than in the Maze. The bears patiently waited for a dog salmon to wiggle in the water. At the slightest hint of such activity, the big animals would thunder through the bay, swatting and pouncing. The success rate here was much higher than with the salmon in the Maze streams.

Virtually every time one of these dark hunters tried, they caught a fish.

The acoustics in the area were superb, like a perfectly designed theater. The bay was surrounded on three sides by a series of green mountains tipped with ice. The combination of ocean and mountains trapped sounds in the Forbidden Zone and made the slightest one audible. Each time a bear caught a fish, a crunching bite rang out across the bay and the seagulls screamed for leftovers. This could be heard from hundreds of yards away as clearly as if I were standing right there among them.

Unsuccessful bears fidgeted with jealousy when others caught a fish. Larger males often took on less dominant bears who had caught fish. Frequently, these dominant bears would chase the successful bears. Most of the time, the chase resulted in a stolen fish. Within minutes, the subordinate would land another fresh fish. Bears do not fight to the death over such matters. The loser of a fish simply shrugs it off and catches more food.

As the tide fell, the bears began to fish in the newly exposed areas. They were so far out it seemed as if they were on their way to Russia. Eventually, I could see that several bears had even traveled to the waters a short distance from my tent. This year I was camped near a creek that emptied into the bay. The lower tides uncovered the creek's flowing outlet, forming a flat larger than any in the Grizzly Sanctuary. The low tides forced me to again crawl on all fours, so I would have a better chance of blending in with the multitude of bears on my way back to the tent.

Long after sunset, the bears continued fishing. I could hear the splash of water as bears thrashed around in pursuit of salmon. Once in a while, the splashing was interrupted by the sounds of eating or the growls of a bear brawl. I went to bed, lulled to sleep by the splashing of bears.

I knew better than to take the Forbidden Zone for granted, but so far, things were going well. There were even more bears than the year before, yet none had been hostile. I really felt that my new strategy was the reason things were progressing so nicely. I was safer this year because, without a boat to protect, I didn't have to camp along the shoreline, and because the salmon had already arrived, sating many of the bears. Coupled with my new tactics, I was learning how to exist with all kinds of grizzlies.

Every bear encounter is different because of the variables in the personalities of both the humans and the bears. The difference between encountering Taffy and encountering Demon is immense. If the human panics during an encounter, the dynamics change and the danger increases. For the most part, bears—even Forbidden Zone bears—mean no harm to people. A slow, calm withdrawal almost always defuses the situation. Because I had chosen to live with wild bears, close encounters were inevitable. It was essential for my survival to correctly interpret a bear's mood and intentions. Still, I'm keenly aware that it takes only a single misinterpretation to get myself killed.

At night, the radio kept me up to speed on events around the world. As usual, the world was up to its ears in murder and mayhem. Most of the affairs of the continental United States and the rest of the world were meaningless to the animals in the Forbidden Zone. Short of a nuclear war, the Forbidden Zone might as well have been another planet. The news that night also reported on a hurricane about to hit the east coast of the United States.

Ironically, while I was out along the bay photographing the bears fishing the next day, winds started to gust from the north. They were warm winds, created by building high pressure. In these parts of Alaska, winds from the north and west generally bring favorable meteorological conditions. So even though it was blowing hard, about forty miles per hour, I was expecting good weather.

Around nine P.M., the gusts increased to about fifty miles per hour, nothing compared to the hurricane I had heard about on the radio the night before. Only slightly concerned by the weather, I placed logs on top of each of the tent's eight spikes. After my peanut butter and jelly dinner, I read for a bit and tried to sleep.

By eleven P.M., the winds were wild. I was smug about having anchored the tent. Such foresight! Such a smart camper! I drifted off to sleep listening to the howling winds.

Such an idiot! At approximately one A.M., all hell broke loose. The winds were more than seventy miles per hour and had reached hurricane force. The winds blew so hard that the tent's frame pushed in, smashing into my face. "Oh, shit," I thought, "I'm in trouble." The noise was deafening; I knew that I had to reinforce the tent's anchors, but I was too frightened to move, and lay there hoping that the winds would just go away. Then I thought about my bear friends. How were Taffy, Snowball, and all the others holding up? By now the winds were easily up to eighty miles per hour. Suddenly the tent's fly blew off, flapping like an old kite.

Between the gusts, there were brief periods of stillness, as if the wind were psyching itself up for the next blow. I left the tent and saw that a half-phase moon lit the wilderness. The tall grasses rippled madly in a naturally choreographed dance; sticks and dry twigs careened off my head; a million whitecaps flickered in the bay. It felt like a massive hallucination, beautiful in a scary way. I managed to retrieve the tent's fly and secure it in place during a lull. Just as I drove the last two pegs into the ground, the wind ripped them out again. One of the sharp metal pegs whistled by my cheek and disappeared into the night. It was as if the Forbidden Zone were possessed. "Fuck you, Forbidden Zone!" I yelled into the wind. "I'm the champion!" I ran around the Forbidden Zone in bare feet, gathering more logs. I gathered pile after pile, stacking them to ballast the tent. The metal frame still pushed into my face, but the tent held. The Forbidden Zone blew its hardest, but I remained.

The next morning was still, serene and sunny, as if nothing had happened. Grizzlies played in the water. Eagles piccoloed sweet songs of joy. My tent looked ridiculous entombed in a fortress of logs.

That afternoon, I crawled back to the bay and into a gathering of bears. As the tide slowly receded, I moved out into the action. Bears within 100 yards of me showed no concern. My strategy was really working.

I watched a beautiful jet-black grizzly who was busy scanning the waters 100 yards away from me. As soon as the bear spotted a fish, it moved toward it through the water, like a dancer. It pounced, and with one swat caught the fish. Just as the black bear started to eat, a large, nasty-looking brown bear charged in, intent on taking the fish. The smaller, darker bear ran for its life with the fish clenched between its teeth. The chase lasted for several minutes, but the aggressor was unrelenting and the dark bear finally dropped the fish, giving in to the larger male. While the dominant bear ate the stolen fish, the darker bear nervously released its bladder. The spray of urine shot backward, so the beautiful dark bear was a female. Leaving the brown male to his feast, she timidly approached me through the water.

She came nearer, one paw poised in the air after each step. Satisfied that I was not a threat, she settled down and fished near me for about an hour. I named her Molly. As she splashed about I took pictures furiously, buoyed by her presence. At times, Molly went into deeper waters. She'd snag a fish and trot back to me, eating it as I congratulated her on her catch. Molly was the first bear to allow me within her personal space in the Forbidden Zone.

The bears working the bay used two of their senses to locate fish. For the most part, they heard the fish caught in the sandbars. Then the bears would find the fish with their eyes and charge. Obviously, their senses of smell, touch, and taste were used when they ate. Occasionally the sequence was broken, which made me wonder about their eyesight. Some salmon had washed up whole on shore, either dead or dying after spawning. Even though the fish made no sound to give away their location, the bears would scan the waters at great distances and spot them. At times, some bears spotted fish a hundred yards away. Bear biologists differ on the subject of bears' sight. Many agree that bears have good eyesight, perhaps 20/20, but have difficulty discerning still objects. They also agree that bears living in open tundra tend to have better eyesight than those living in thick forests. The bears of the Forbidden Zone appeared to have excellent eyesight, and were able to see stationary objects like the fish and myself.

Molly had an amazing sense of sight. Time and time again, as the tide fell, a spent salmon washed up on shore, floundering on the flats. It would be barely alive, slowly opening and closing its mouth. Molly certainly couldn't hear the fish, and at a distance of 200 yards, I couldn't believe she'd see it. Then Molly would look toward the fish and stalk right up to it. Molly would grasp the writhing salmon with her right paw, then decapitate it with a confident bite. She would then strip off the skin, slurp it down, and finish by eating her favorite parts. While I watched, Molly caught eleven dog salmon. The average dog salmon weighed between eight and fifteen pounds, and Molly had consumed at least seven pounds of each fish per catch, which meant that she'd eaten at least seventy-seven pounds of fish in just over an hour. I was sure Molly had caught other fish before I'd arrived. Without a doubt, Molly had eaten over a hundred pounds of fish on this August day. While I watched, Molly caught her twelfth fish, excreted a large pile of waste, and stretched out on a sandbar to take a well-deserved nap.

Later that evening, a mother bear with two spring cubs woke me from an early sleep. They were fishing in the creek in front of my tent. Each time the mother landed a fish, the cubs let out a foghorn call, demanding a bite. They were making such a racket that I couldn't sleep, so I crept out to watch. Besides the family, there were six other bears fishing, including Molly. That bear was insatiable! Molly reconfirmed what I already knew about grizzlies:

They must take advantage of all food sources when they are available.

Every moment in the Forbidden Zone showed me something important about bears, yet one incident with an impact that will stay with me for the rest of my life happened on the same day I watched Molly gorge on salmon.

An unusually large adult female, accompanied by her plump yearling, began to fish in a creek just in front of my tent. Within minutes each had caught two fish, one after the other. Their splashing caught the attention of a male bear, who emerged from a nearby thicket of alder bushes. He was in even worse shape than Mickey had been when I found him this year in the Grizzly Sanctuary. Most of his ribs showed through his fur and he dragged his hind legs, which were obviously broken or severely injured. Though he wasn't more than ten—the prime of life for a grizzly— he was in desperate condition. I wanted so much to help him, but there was nothing that could be done. Natural selection had made the Forbidden Zone a perfectly balanced ecosystem long before my arrival. Perhaps this bear's passing would help another bear's survival.

As the healthy mother and yearling caught fish after fish, it was all the injured bear could do to drag his body to the creek and collapse along its bank. Suddenly, the mother caught sight of him and walked toward the weakened male. He struggled to get up and move away from the dominant bear. My heart was in my mouth as the mother approached the impaired bear. "Please don't hurt him," I wished. She walked directly up to him, and delicately kissed and caressed his face, lavishing him with love and attention. The infirm bear relished the care with heavy, blinking eyes. It was the most beautiful few minutes of my life. As she walked away, the male noticed a pile of nearly whole, discarded fish that the mother bear had left behind. He limped over and ate the fish. Did the mother bear purposely leave the gift for the injured male? Only she knew the answer. For so long, people have thought of bears as cruel, unfeeling animals. But I know differently. The bears know differently. Miracles happen in the Forbidden Zone.

It was very difficult for me to tell just how many bears lived in the Forbidden Zone. There were definitely not as many as in the Grizzly Sanctuary. My best guess was that there were 100 different bears that made their way through the Forbidden Zone during the spring, summer, and fall. I was very impressed with the large number of mothers with cubs. During my stay, I saw two mothers with single spring cubs, four sets of twin spring cubs, three pairs of yearlings, one mother and a yearling, and two mothers with single two-year-olds. I saw a total of nineteen offspring in the Forbidden Zone.

In all, I had seen forty to fifty cubs of various ages during my studies in 1995, and not one cub had been killed by a male bear. In fact, after years of studying and living among wild brown grizzlies, I had never seen an incident of infanticide. There is no doubt that infanticide occurs among bears; it is a natural factor of bear behavior, and results in a stronger population. However, I believe that infanticide among bears has been greatly exaggerated by people.

The fishing activity was dwindling in the Forbidden Zone. Each day, fewer and fewer fish spawned in the waters, and the number of bears fishing dropped noticeably. For the most part, the bears simply soaked in the bay's waters, cooling off during the extended heat wave, but I knew that this was a temporary lull. Expert fishermen like Rex had informed me that in these waters, the peak runs of chum salmon occurred later in August and September. The bears were merely waiting, knowing full well that the fish would return.

Each day, as bears fished a bit and played in the water, I crawled across the Forbidden Zone and sat in the open along the shores of the bay. As long as I stayed on all fours, I was accepted by the bears as they fished. Bears passed by sporadically, yet aside from Molly, I didn't have a relationship with any other grizzlies in the Forbidden Zone.

Molly came out and sat down within forty feet of me, obviously comfortable with my close presence. As Molly sat nearby, other bears came around to look me over. One young bear approached, then sucked up a big huff of air. He woofed, stood on his hind legs, and trotted away in concern. Obviously, he didn't like what he smelled. Another young bear approached from behind, and sniffed loudly as well. He reacted by stomping his paws into the wet sand. I remained calm, though my presence was clearly being protested. I decided to speak to the bear. "Easy, little buddy," I said. "No one's going to hurt you." The bear looked at me quizzically, then calmed down and walked away.

I'd been in the Forbidden Zone for nearly a week when I spotted a large male fishing far out in the bay, a good quarter mile away. I sat and observed, a camera perched on a tripod in front of me. For no discernible reason, the bear began to slowly move through the water in my direction. Every hundred yards or so it stopped, to either concentrate on fishing or on me. At seventy-five yards, it was time for me to start considering my options. As usual, there were three: I could withdraw and pray that he didn't view it as a sign of weakness and charge; I could just remain seated and hope he would turn away; or I could leap up demonstratively. I decided to just sit quietly and hope for the best.

The massive chocolate bear closed to within fifty feet of me. His body language didn't signal aggression or distress. However, bears like Demon had taught me not to trust nonchalant behavior. The grizzly's jaw hung crookedly, giving him a menacing look. A large raw wound gaped on his left side, which meant he was probably a fighting bear. He came closer, until I could feel the vibration of his weight through the sand. I tried to snap a couple of photographs without being pushy. He stopped within thirty feet of me, sniffed the air like the others had, then moved on majestically. His keen senses told him that although I wasn't a bear, I certainly wasn't a threat. Fifty feet farther on, he plopped to the wet, sandy ground and napped. I lay back and soaked up some rays, sharing a nap in the August sun with the crooked-jaw grizzly.

In the evenings at the Forbidden Zone, I wrote in my journal, or read. For some reason, I was picking up an alternative rock station on my radio. At night, I usually listened softly to news and talk radio, keeping one ear open for bear visits. But since the bears were fishing away from my tent, I took advantage of the New Wave sounds and indulged myself with a bit more volume for a few evenings. On the third night, the music fizzled into static. I decided to forget the sounds of civilization altogether and absorb the sounds of the wild.

Immediately, I heard the unmistakable sounds of bears in the neighborhood. I stepped into the evening and sat outside the tent for hours. In the dim light, bears moved by at staggered intervals. There were big bears, little bears, mothers with cubs, funny-looking bears, and beautiful bears like Molly. Some splashed along the nearby creek, while others passed fifty yards in front of the tent. Others were so close that I could almost stretch out my hand and touch them. Each had its own agenda, and paid me no mind. After a while, I realized that during this lazy, unscheduled evening of casual observation, I'd seen more bears around my tent than ever before. I was so thankful that I'd turned off the radio. The sights and sounds of their simple lives were so much better than drums and guitars.

My stay at the Forbidden Zone was growing short. Soon my friend Rex would stop by and move me to a fourth study location. It was an area I had visited before, but never camped in. As I thought about Expedition '95, it seemed strange that the safest bears to be around, so far, were those of the Forbidden Zone. I hoped that the bears in the next spot would be as kind.

I was preparing to take a farewell hike to the far side of the bay when a mother with two yearlings appeared in the distance, heading toward my creek. They were nearly a mile away, giving me plenty of time to set up my cameras on a camouflaged ridge. A few hundred yards away, a large male bear was asleep in the sun. He was sleeping so soundly that I didn't expect him to be disturbed by the oncoming family or by me. The mother walked her cubs from left to right across the creek while I fired away with the Minolta. The big male remained asleep. Then, without warning, Timber, the bear with the crooked jaw, showed up, effectively sandwiching the sleeping male between himself and the mother with cubs. I spotted the pending disaster before any of the bears did. Sensing trouble, the big male sprang to his feet and moved to his left, away from the mother and toward Timber. Timber responded with a quick, nasty, hop charge, sending the rival male running. The poor guy had just been napping, minding his own business, when BAM, he awoke to a confrontation. To avoid the smaller bear, the mother moved into Timber's space, huffing and popping her jaws so loudly the sound echoed throughout the Zone. Timber stopped, allowing her to sweep up her cubs and bolt.

Meanwhile, the displaced subordinate male was angrily walking toward the shore, taking a path that would carry him right over my chest. He saw me, and decided to vent his frustration over being rudely awakened and displaced. His ice-cold eyes locked with mine, his ears swept back, and his head dropped into the fighting position. I moved forward, emitting a strong, guttural, "Hey! Hey! Hey!" He retreated, walked around the ridge, then popped up out of the thicket like an attacking shark. Ramming his head through the grass and clacking his fangs, he came toward me again.

"Okay, boy, you've had a bad day," I sympathized. "You've been jerked around royally, but that's no reason to take it out on me."

The bear grimaced. Long, sharp teeth hung in front of my face. "You may not realize it, but I totally understand what you've been through. Now just relax and we'll call it even." He backed up a bit and angrily began eating. "Come on, fellow, don't stay in that foul mood." The bear turned around and briskly walked away.

Timber, the mom, and the sleeping bear may not have learned anything from the confrontation, but I sure did. In the wilderness, you can't take anything for granted. You can be killed on your last day just as easily as on your first. There's no coasting in the wild. The bears never get to coast, and neither do I.

Throughout my last evening in the Forbidden Zone, the grizzlies splashed through the nearby creek. The sound was comforting, like ocean waves, and lulled me to sleep. In my dreams I soared above the grizzlies, protecting the bears below.

My final day in the Forbidden Zone was perfect. The temperature was in the low seventies, a mild breeze blew, and the sky was bright and clear. I planned a four-hour hike, but the surroundings were so pleasant that I stayed out twice as long. I stumbled over some fresh moose prints and cursed my luck. Aside from Timmy the Fox and family, I'd rarely seen any other animals in the Alaskan wilderness. I found wolverine prints, river otter and lynx prints, but never their makers. It wasn't just bad luck. First, I always camped near Alaska's top predator, which kept all the other creatures at bay. Second, I was focused on bears. It was disappointing in a way, but I couldn't really be sad. I was closer to the grizzlies than other species cared to be.

On the farewell hike, my luck changed. Coming out of the mountains, and along the grassy coast, I spied a mother moose with a single calf. They were too far away for a photo, so I just sat and observed for a while, congratulating myself on finally seeing a moose. They were right in the middle of an area with a lot of grizzly activity, and I was a bit concerned for them, although grizzlies usually hunt moose calves in the spring. At this time of year, the mother moose probably knew that the bears were more interested in fish than in her calf. Still, I said a little prayer for their safe passage through the Forbidden Zone.

The vast seaside mud flats in the area where I walked were covered with a mosaic of bear paw prints. Thousands of tracks were embedded, from tiny cub prints to monstrous, dinosaur-sized ones. The grizzly footprints were nature's photographs, recording impressions of something grand remaining on earth.

The waters of the creek near my tent began to ripple with spawning salmon. The bears began to perk up and take notice. Eager to get more photos, I scrambled through the mud toward a good vantage point. I reached the creek on the south bank, right in line with the approaching bears. Realizing that I might disturb them, I crossed to the other side and hunkered down on all fours on the muddy bank.

Two opposing male bears began to splash furiously through the water in search of salmon. The smaller of the two was more proficient, landing fish after fish. The larger bear chased the smaller in an attempt to steal its fresh catch. A cops and robbers chase went on wildly, only in this case, the robber pursued the cop. The smaller bear did not give up, and finally found a safe haven in the distant alders. The would-be thief returned to the creek in a surly mood, kicking and stomping the mud. In the next hour, the smaller bear caught nine salmon. The hapless larger bear snagged only two.

Toward the end of the fishing session, a shaggy blondish bear, about three years old, joined the pair. At first glance, I thought it was a wolf. Its size and doglike physique were uncanny. Though the dog-bear was smaller, it fished peacefully with the other males.

The fishing ended for the trio when Timber plodded out onto the mud flat. Attracted by the splashing of the other bears, Timber stalked in their direction. Once again, that put Timber, the bear with the crooked jaw, on a course with me. There was no need to panic, but I did need to make room. I crawled out of the mud into the creek below. Timber strolled right by me without a hint of aggression. Timber had fish to catch, and I welcomed the chance to clean up.

The three bears scooted off in different directions, away from Timber. Timber made a few halfhearted attempts to catch fish, but was unsuccessful. It seemed to me that the three bears could probably have stayed on and fished safely next to Timber, but perhaps they knew better than I did.

The social hierarchy of bears was always of special interest to me. Here in the Forbidden Zone, it was apparent that Timber was the dominant bear. For the most part, the largest bears were at the top of the ladder. I wondered if those large bears became alpha bears simply by being big, or if they had to earn it by battling their way up. The majority of the dominant bears I had seen were of stable disposition and were relatively free of scars. Timber had one moderate wound on his left side, and his crooked jaw was probably the result of a past altercation. Yet overall, he looked as fit as a fiddle. In the Grizzly Sanctuary, each large dominant male was in showroom condition. Hulk, Garth, Mr. Chocolate, and the king of kings, Czar, all had splendid physiques and calm temperaments. There was no doubt in my mind that the safest bear to be around was one of the giant males in these legally nonhunted areas.

My photo studies on the final day in the Forbidden Zone really capped off my stay. As I left the creek, I finally stood on two legs. I bowed in thanks to Timber and the other grizzlies, because the bears of the Forbidden Zone had taught me a very important lesson.

I had come here in fear, determined to survive within a group of ferocious, secretive animals. I crawled around on all fours, afraid to walk upright and show my true self. Yet no bears had charged, no bears had been really aggressive, no bears cared if I stayed. I stood among them now, humbled that they had accepted me.

12

Rex arrived right on schedule to take me to my next study area—the G Spot. I called it the G Spot for the many grizzlies and the beautiful glacier that dominated the landscape; it just may have been one of the prettiest places in Alaska. The massive glacier loomed above everything, the blue of its ice contrasting sharply with the dark peaks of the surrounding mountains, towering over green fields and clear bays and creeks. The G Spot had a swiftly moving creek that branched off into a delta as it emptied into the bay, which was the reason for the number of grizzlies. Like the Forbidden Zone, the G Spot hosted spawning dog salmon in August and September. Three grizzlies were fishing as I arrived.

I unloaded my gear and decided to camp in one of the few level, dry places. As I set everything up, a 1,000-pound grizzly strolled by, only 25 feet away. The three fishing bears watched me at work, then went back to their prey. After I was through I crawled into my tent and tried to sleep, anxious about what the morning would bring.

In the morning, I sat on the creek bank and marveled at the

view. According to a topographical map, the glacier and mountain located at the end of the G Spot was 6,000 feet high. A thick forest of alder bushes and a creek at its base made it accessible only to wild animals. I used my binoculars for a closer inspection. Within the sandy creek delta was a nice patch of sedge grass. By now, the browning sedge was well past its peak nutritional value, but the bears still nibbled at it. The thick wads of old, dried sedge eaten by the bears worked in their digestive tract. As this point in the season, the large amounts of fish they ate could contain tapeworms. Forced through their intestines, the old sedge grass flushed out the worms.

A mother with two spring cubs was out, giving me a warm feeling. A huge, dark-coated male entered the pasture from behind a curtain of alders. I did a double take and focused in. Could it be? Here? I couldn't be positive from that distance, but it sure looked like my old friend Mr. Chocolate. I'd spent five summers with Mr. C. since our first encounter in his daybed. Was he really here? It was possible. The G Spot was twenty miles from the Grizzly Sanctuary as the crow flies. Each year, in late July, Mr. C. would migrate to some other habitat, and it was well within the realm of possibility that he'd come here. I was thrilled because Mr. C. always seemed to be nearby when I was in trouble. Time and time again I had dodged an overactive young subadult by heading for Mr. C. He'd always obliged, chasing the adolescent away. If he truly was here, my stay was going to be super.

The big bear was grazing on sedge grass, surprisingly near the mother and cubs. That raised my hopes, because in the Sanctuary, Mr. C. grazed peacefully alongside all the bears and created no tension. Which isn't to say that he didn't command respect. For reasons I've never fully understood, even bigger bears like Czar and Garth never pushed Mr. Chocolate.

A half hour later, a medium-sized grizzly appeared. The male was five to seven years old, and weighed about five hundred pounds. Yet this time, the mother bear panicked and would not tolerate the intruder. She stood, huffing and popping her jaw, then led her cubs across the creek and into the thick cover. The big chocolate bear looked up, then continued eating. If this wasn't Mr. C., it had to be his twin brother.

The young male proceeded to scout the creeks for fish. It was high tide, so the water was too deep for fishing. If any salmon were there, they were hidden in the deep. The male stretched out on his tummy, paws supporting his heavy head, and napped, no doubt waiting for the salmon to start running.

With little going on, I took a walk and came across a hillside covered with salmonberry bushes. The salmonberry, *Rubus spectabilis*, is a member of the rose family, but lives for only two seasons. "Rubus" means bramble, and "spectabilis" means exceptionally showy. The Eskimos called them "muck-a-muck." Bears don't care what they're called, they just eat as many as possible. The berries start out bright reddish purple, then ripen to an orange gold, and bloom on thick, seven-foot bushes. The raspberrylike fruits are the size of a human thumb. I made a mental note to return to this lovely hill to try and photograph some bears eating the berries, which are a vital part of their diet.

Circling back to camp, I ducked inside the tent for a nap. I didn't get the chance to rest for long before some wild splashing jolted me awake. In bare feet, I stepped out into an astonishing spectacle. The combination of a falling tide and a rush of spawning salmon had transformed a quiet day into complete madness. Eight bears raced through the creek, the waters pulsing with fish. I put on my shoes and gathered up my cameras, ready to join the feast.

In the adjacent creek, a frosted-blond adult female caught salmon with great dexterity. She had a beautiful platinum coat and a silly stubby tail that bounced as she galloped along. I quickly named her Sugarbear. Because the tide fell rapidly, her work was made easier as an increasing number of fish ran aground. Sugarbear strained to detect the floundering salmon. The moment a fish gave up its position, she was off, racing in pursuit of her catch. With every stride, water sprayed out of the creek. Within seconds, she'd pinned a fish in the water, clamped her teeth on it, and hiked to dry land.

Other bears bolted through the water, also enjoying great success. However, after an hour, it became clear that Sugarbear was the best fisher. All seven of the other fishing bears were male, ranging in age from late adolescence to older, larger adults.

Over the years I've found interesting behavioral patterns regarding food procurement. Given an equal chance, single adult females were the most adept at securing different foods. At the clam flats, Booble, Saturn, and Holly were superior clam diggers, particularly during mating years. Fishing standouts included Melissa, Kate, Molly, Snowball, and now Sugarbear. Why was that? It was odd that the giant males weren't better, considering that they needed a lot more calories to support their substantially larger frames. Perhaps it was because those female bears were preparing to give birth in their winters' dens and were stocking up in preparation for the caloric demands of potential offspring. I believe that this was the reason, but I need to continue my detailed field studies and seek assistance from as many qualified bear biologists as possible.

Meanwhile, as Sugarbear continued to catch fish, the success rate of the seven males plummeted. As a result, a few of the dominant males followed Sugarbear and stole her catch. She seemed to shrug it off as a cost of doing business, but eventually, she took her catches farther away and ate in peace.

A large, dark male stepped out of the tall grass behind me. It was the same large male I'd spotted earlier in the sedge grass field. I really hoped that it was Mr. Chocolate. He walked by slowly, stepping out into the creek bed, giving me a chance to take a good, long look. There was no doubt it was my big chocolate friend.

"Mr. Chocolate!" I yelled. "Mr. Chocolate, you don't know how good it is to see you." Mr. Chocolate sat down and stared back at me. "Now, don't let me interfere and keep you from your fishing duties," I said to him. "We'll have lots of time to socialize later." Mr. Chocolate got up and headed to the creek.

Mr. Chocolate wasn't pushy at all, yet every other bear moved out of his way as he approached. I felt like a proud parent, beaming at my child's dominance on the playing field. But my pride was deflated as I watched the big bear in action. Mr. Chocolate caught fewer fish than just about every other bear. After an hour or so he gravitated toward Sugarbear, possibly hoping that she had a better fishing spot. He didn't steal a single fish from Sugarbear as she landed catch after catch. Satisfied that he wasn't a thief, she began to trust the bigger bear. Mr. C. only caught one fish for every two or three that Sugarbear got. That wasn't too bad, considering that Sugarbear was a fishing superstar. She was really good, sometimes even batting live fish from the creek onto the banks. I'd heard of that technique before, but I hadn't seen it until this day in the G Spot. Sugarbear continued to catch fish, leaving plenty of leftovers for Mr. Chocolate. Mr. C. put no pressure on Sugarbear to surrender the fish. He just waited casually until she had eaten her favorite parts and had moved on to other prey. The observation made me wonder if Sugarbear and Mr. Chocolate were consciously working together. She landed the fish, and he protected her from the thieving bears, receiving a portion of the profits for his services. After nine cooperative efforts, I felt that there might be some substance to my theory.

On his own, Mr. Chocolate had a funny way of fishing. He sauntered through the creek, and after every other step, he slapped at the water with his left paw. His mouth was open in deep concentration, pink tongue hanging askew. Most of Mr. Chocolate's spirited slaps resulted in bubbles, but occasionally he'd scare some fish into a frenzy. Then, he'd spring into action and catch a salmon. Mr. Chocolate didn't have the luxury of eating only the tastiest parts of the fish. He was really big, and he wasn't catching as much as most of the other bears. After Mr. Chocolate ate a fish, there wasn't a single morsel left behind. Scavenger birds landed, expecting their share. They shrieked in protest when there was nothing left. "Hey, show my buddy some respect, you sleazebags!" I yelled down at the birds.

Later during the day's fishing, I did something that may have teetered on the brink of acceptable ethical standards. Mr. Chocolate had positioned himself directly in front of me. Occasionally he caught his own salmon, but for the most part, he was depending on Sugarbear's scraps. Every other bear was doing great, and I was a trifle embarrassed for my longtime friend. After floundering for a bit, Mr. Chocolate moved farther upstream. The instant he left, several fish got jammed in the immediate creek, right in front of me. The salmon were exhausted, and would be easy prey, already half dead, washed up on the sandy bank of the waters. If only Mr. Chocolate could see these fish. Even he could catch these. Without a second thought, I decided to help Mr. Chocolate. "Hey, Mr. Chocolate! Hey, Mr. Chocolate, looky here! Fresh salmon! Come and get it!" I yelled. Mr. C. looked quizzically at me. Then I chucked a rock into the creek near the dying fish, so that the splash of the rock imitated the sound of a spawning salmon. He stepped a few paces closer, looking extremely interested. I tossed a second and third rock, until Mr. Chocolate charged across the muddy flat. As the half-ton grizzly approached the creek, he suddenly stopped, skidding several yards to the edge. For a moment, Mr. Chocolate looked delighted with his cool slide. Then back to business, Mr. Chocolate dove into the creek and onto the fish. He smacked one fish with a right paw, and another with a giant left. Mortally wounded, the two fish wriggled, one under each of his paws. It was the first and only time I'd ever seen a bear catch two fish simultaneously. Mr. Chocolate quickly killed each fish with powerful bites. Then he methodically ate the fish one by one, leaving not so much as a fin for the birds squawking above his head.

I sat only thirty feet away, watching and photographing the entire event. Mr. Chocolate paused between bites and gazed up toward me, not concerned at all by my presence as he ate. We had certainly met under rather dubious circumstances on that day he caught me sleeping in his bear bed, yet throughout the years, Mr. Chocolate had not only tolerated my presence, but seemed to enjoy it.

I was fairly positive that Mr. Chocolate did not associate his salmon catch with my rock-throwing signals. However, without my tip-off, the salmon would surely have washed into the bay and become food for something else. It seemed the least I could have done for a bear that had provided me with years of valuable research information, and even a little friendship.

The fishing session had begun around three P.M., and was sputtering out by nine. One by one, all nine bears retired. I returned to the tent, exhausted yet fulfilled by a day jammed with excitement. Though my tent was pitched in an area many bears frequented, I felt very safe. Normally, just camping in a new area would be sufficient cause for me to sleep with one eye open. However, I was also reassured by the presence of Mr. Chocolate. After a bit of writing, I fell into a deep, luxurious sleep, and awoke in the morning invigorated. In the nearby creek, bears had begun fishing in the low morning tide. Barefoot as usual, I stepped out to peek at their work. Just a stride from the front flap sat a pile of fresh bear scat. Next to the droppings, the high grass was crushed flat from the weight of an animal. During the night, one of the bears had bedded down close to the tent. I wasn't concerned at all. In fact, I was honored. I hoped that the sleeping bear had been Mr. Chocolate.

Only ten days remained in this season's expedition among the grizzlies. I was not only safe among them, but I felt like a healthy, complete animal. Why would I want to return to human civilization? This was truly my home. How could I leave?

Once again, the tide dictated the actions of the grizzlies. The early morning's low tide exposed spawning salmon, bringing out several hungry bears. As the higher tides came, the bears left the creeks to take naps or graze on the grass. By midafternoon, the cycle reversed, and the bears rematerialized. Obviously the bears knew which tide had more fish because more participated in the later session.

The afternoon fishing frenzy was in full swing. I was beginning to be familiar with the bears that regularly fished nearby: Besides Mr. Chocolate and Sugarbear, there were four other grizzlies.

There was Wizard, a young, golden-brown male of about 600 pounds. He was gregarious, and an excellent fisher. He reminded me of a puppy, with a lean body and immense paws. I had a feeling that Wizard was going to be a big bear.

Next there was Whisper. His coloring was similar to Wizard's, but he wasn't nearly as large. Whisper was shy around most of the bears, but seemed to get along just fine with Wizard. Whisper was an unassuming bear who never stole fish from anyone.

There was also a giant, blondish bear, perhaps nine feet long and weighing a thousand pounds, that I named Crate. Crate, like Mr. Chocolate, didn't catch as many fish as Wizard or Sugarbear. However, Crate was a big thief. He stalked around the creek, keeping an eye on everything, intent on taking whatever he could from the younger, smaller bears.

The fourth bear was a bit smaller than Crate, and auburn in color. I named him Clay. He shared Crate's surly attitude and was a bandit as well.

Crate usually worked a second creek that flowed across an exposed tide flat. Clay also worked in the far creek most of the time. Sugarbear and Mr. Chocolate usually fished in the creek adjacent to my tent. Wizard and Whisper moved back and forth between the two creeks. When Crate and Clay were on a stealing rampage, Wizard and Whisper also stayed at the creek near my campsite and fished peacefully.

Sugarbear began to catch a streak of salmon, which got Crate's attention. Crate's own fishing efforts had failed, and there wasn't a bear close enough that he could quickly steal from. He crossed the flat into Sugarbear's personal space. Meanwhile, Mr. Chocolate approached Sugarbear's rear, hoping to resume his habit of eating her leftovers. As Crate closed in, it looked like big trouble. The bears were similar in size, but Crate's surly manner seemed to give him the dominant edge. The moment Sugarbear landed another fish, Crate charged in to steal it. Mr. Chocolate calmly stepped forward and intercepted the thief. Crate's aggression abruptly ceased: He bowed his head in submission, then nervously looked away. Mr. Chocolate coolly turned his back in a display of dominance. Crate trotted away, and didn't bother Sugarbear again while she was with Mr. Chocolate. Mr. Chocolate was truly an amazing bear. He was gentle, yet sometime during his life he had earned the respect he commanded.

Minutes after the confrontation, I spotted a new bear heading toward me along the shoreline. He was huge and dark, similar in appearance to Mr. Chocolate. His course along the beach promised that he would collide with me if I didn't act quickly. When the giant closed to within thirty feet, I attempted to interpret his body language. He did not seem stressed or aggressive, so when he got to within twenty feet, I stood up and spoke gently, trying to offer him access to the beach by slowly backing away. The giant bear was startled and froze in his tracks. The next few seconds would determine my fate. If this was a rare "Demon" bear, my life could be over. The bear stared and sniffed in my direction for a few agonizing seconds.

"It's OK, big bear," I said softly. "I'm a good animal." The dark giant quickly compromised and stepped gingerly around me to get to the salmon creek. As it turned out, the dark bear had a lovely disposition, and ate only his own fish. I decided to name him Duffy.

Hours passed as I observed the feeding. I kept a scorecard of caught and eaten fish. The roster of bears included Mr. Chocolate, Sugarbear, Wizard, Crate, Whisper, and Clay. Duffy was also now in the lineup. Over a period of five hours, Sugarbear caught twenty-two fish and ate sixteen. The other six were stolen when she was near Crate and Clay without Mr. Chocolate. Wizard caught nineteen fish, but lost three to Crate. Crate caught five fish, but also stole and ate another seven. Whisper caught twelve fish and only lost one to Crate. Duffy caught seven fish and seemed content. Clay caught seven, but stole six more. Mr. Chocolate caught just six fish, but cleaned up nearly ten of Sugarbear's.

A few other bears wandered in and out of the action. This included a small, paranoid subadult, another larger subadult, and the mother with two spring cubs I had seen a few times before. Due to Crate's aggressive behavior, none of these bears seemed to trust the overall situation.

The late August light was starting to fade behind the glacier around nine P.M., and it was completely gone by ten-thirty. Darkness meant the approach of autumn in the land of the grizzlies. Their coats were already beginning to fill out noticeably in preparation for the long, cold night that was coming.

I lay awake, reading into the evening. People are always giving me books about bears, and I liked to browse through them in my tent. This book was all about a man and his passion for killing bears. With each page, I shook with increasing rage. In detail, the book explained how to kill bears, including baiting and trapping techniques. It was riddled with graphic photographs of slaughtered bears and their smiling killers. My stomach heaved at the sight of the hunters flaunting the corpses of beautiful bears. To end the life of such a magnificent animal for nothing more than a trophy or a thrill is despicable.

It was finally dark, and I was still riled up about the murder of bears throughout the world. Suddenly, I felt the ground start to vibrate from the paws of a big bear. Then I heard the swish and crush of tall grass being trampled. A bear was bedding down for the evening. Without alarm I left the tent, shining my flashlight into the pitch-black evening. Gradually, I maneuvered the bright light in the direction of the visitor. I caught sight of a gigantic pile of dark-brown fur and the supernatural glow of illuminated eyes. Mr. Chocolate, my beautiful friend, had stopped by to spend the night.

I immediately turned off the light and sat down in the damp grass. I was troubled by my thoughts about bear hunters, and sought solace from Mr. Chocolate. "Mr. Chocolate," I said, "you and all of the bears have been such a wonderful inspiration to me. You have given me so much peace and hope. You have taught me to be dependable and responsible. I try so hard to be decent and good, but I've still got a long way to go. Tonight I've been reading about animal killers. Many people would love to kill you, Mr. Chocolate. I'm ashamed to be human! I want to be like you, wild and free, liberated from the wicked ways of people."

My eyes had adjusted to the dim evening light. Mr. Chocolate lay sprawled out on his tummy, a dozen feet away, with his head supported by the backsides of both paws. His eyes were closed for most of the talk, but opened up sporadically, twinkling in the starlight. His breaths were long and tranquil. For eons, people have called these animals dangerous beasts. They have always been wrong. It is humans who are the most dangerous of beasts.

"Mr. Chocolate, I will try to teach people about the beautiful lives of bears. I will ask the hunters to find room in their hearts to let you live in peace. Until I succeed, I'll watch over you," I said to the giant bear. "Good night, big fellow, and sleep tight. We're gonna have a great day tomorrow." With that, I crawled back inside my tent and into the warmth of the sleeping bag, listening to Mr. Chocolate snore right outside my tent.

The next thing I knew it was seven-thirty in the morning, and Mr. Chocolate and several other bears were back at work in the intertidal creeks. They weren't concerned about hunters, social injustice, or war, only about living in harmony on earth.

The overcast morning gave way to hazy afternoon sun. Sugarbear waited patiently for some action, sitting on her rump, staring into the creek. The day seemed just right for a cold creek bath. I waded out into the water in my swimming suit. Sugarbear watched from across the creek, her eyes wide with interest. She'd never seen me swim before. I bobbed my head in and out of the chilly, slowly flowing creek. "Whew!" I gasped. "It's freezing in here, Sugarbear!" I said to the captivated bear. "You certainly are a tough girl to handle this frigid water!"

Drying off from my bath, I watched Wizard get a jump on the afternoon fishing. Wizard employed an original technique. He entered the headwaters of the creek, and rode the current. Sitting upright, Wizard whisked through the water with just his face and neck above the surface. Sugarbear did a double take. She decided to go over for a closer look. Wizard washed downstream, then suddenly launched himself out of the creek, a writhing fish clamped between his teeth. Amazed, Sugarbear's eyes nearly popped out of her head!

The sound of Wizard eating his salmon caught the attention of the other bears. From out of nowhere, bears came from the alders onto the banks of the creek. Crate, Whisper, and Clay lined up across from me on the opposite side of the swift creek, determined to investigate the action. Meanwhile, Sugarbear, Mr. Chocolate, and Duffy emerged from behind me and sat down across the water from the other bears.

Wizard ran back upstream and dropped into the swift current. Wizard sailed by the gallery of animal spectators, from bear to bird, and they followed his every move. Once again, Wizard stopped in midstream, abruptly yanking another fish from the creek. The audience was most impressed. How did he do it? The bears were puzzled, and so was I. Then I figured out what Wizard was doing. Since the tide had not fallen enough for standard shallow fishing, Wizard washed down the creek in a sitting position. His long body acted like a shield, deflecting the fish below. Once the salmon underwater collided with his body, Wizard deftly trapped the fish against his chest and locked his jaws onto them.

Crate still wasn't sure how Wizard caught the fish, but he had ideas of his own. He promptly walked over and stole Wizard's catch. Wizard shook it off without concern, and started over once again. Only this time, Wizard solved the thievery problem by riding the current all the way out to the safety of the bay. Then he ate, safe in the deep water.

The rest of the bears were confused. The waters were still too deep for standard fishing. They were all stymied, except for Sugarbear. She boldly imitated Wizard's strategy, and shot the rapids. It must not have been as simple as it appeared, for downstream, poor Sugarbear began to spin out of control. Her mouth hung open, her eyes darting around in panic. She washed up into the bay, empty pawed but not defeated. She hiked back upstream through the other bears and tried again. This time, Sugarbear had ironed out the steering problem and she caught a fish within seconds. For good measure, she improved on Wizard's system by landing on the opposite side of the bank from Crate, safely near Mr. Chocolate.

Mr. Chocolate also attempted to ride the river, but ran into a different problem. Mr. Chocolate was much bigger than Wizard or Sugarbear, and stuck on the creek bottom. However, by this time the tide had fallen to a level where all the bears could participate in the fishing activities. Mr. Chocolate uncorked himself from the creek and resumed his standard fishing technique.

I wondered if Sugarbear had learned Wizard's creek-riding technique through direct observation. If this was true, it was further proof of the great intelligence of brown grizzly bears. Furthermore, the complexity of Wizard's technique was in itself a marvel. It represented a major behavioral find for me, for I had never before seen such a unique fishing strategy. It was my hope that in future years I would find the answer to this question and other secrets by living among the grizzlies.

Mr. Chocolate and Sugarbear had been working together successfully, and did not notice another jam of exhausted salmon near me. Even though he was doing pretty well, I didn't think that Mr. C. was getting enough food for his size, so I began flinging stones into the creek in rapid succession. Both Mr. Chocolate and Sugarbear detected the splashing signals. Sugarbear began to run toward the salmon, her pert, stubby tail wiggling with excitement, Mr. Chocolate following close behind like a huge, dark shadow. Sugarbear lit into the fish, pinning one beneath her right paw. Bobbing her head down, she pulled the salmon from the creek and whisked it away for a private meal. Mr. Chocolate plowed into the fish next, setting off waves with his ample bulk. In fifteen minutes, Mr. Chocolate devoured three whole fish, once again leaving very little for the birds. Sugarbear moved off to other prosperous waters.

I sat in plain sight and watched the salmon attempt to spawn as hungry bears hunted them. The battle here for salmon had a history as long as the ancient practice of clamming in the Grizzly Sanctuary. However, the stakes for the fishing bears were much greater, perhaps even life or death. The primary reason the brown coastal grizzlies are so large is the mass availability of fish to feed on. For many of these brown grizzlies, over half of their body fat comes from their intake of salmon, and a bear that did not get enough fish might not survive. Due to the seriousness of fishing, I never intentionally disrupted the bears' activity in any way. I was happy to just sit in the open with them, observing and photographing.

The run diminished at the day's end, and the bears left. I was busy breaking down my camera equipment and shoving it into the tent when I noticed a grizzly coming closer. It was Wizard. He sat twenty feet from my doorstep and began preening. "Wizard, that water toboggan style of yours is one of the most marvelous fishing techniques I've ever witnessed. Did you figure it out yourself, or did your mother teach you?"

As I spoke to Wizard, Sugarbear approached from behind the tent. She sat down about twenty feet from me and roughly thirty feet from Wizard. Then Whisper walked by the front of the tent, paused momentarily, and headed to the beach. I was starting to shake because the visitors were getting a little too close.

It wasn't over yet. As Wizard and Sugarbear rested, watching my every move, Duffy and Mr. Chocolate headed over. Duffy walked by first, then headed for the beach. He stopped at the sand along the bay and dug a makeshift bed. As Duffy settled in, he positioned himself so that he could watch me as well. Next, Mr. Chocolate sat down against a log about fifteen feet in front of the tent. I was now completely surrounded. Wizard was to the north, Sugarbear to the east, Duffy to the south, and Mr. Chocolate in front, due west. Whisper was farther away, but still in the vicinity. The only bears not in attendance were tough guys Crate and Clay. Why were all of these bears so close to me? Was it random coincidence? Was it curiosity? I hoped that they simply wanted my company. I would be lying if I said that I wasn't intimidated, yet none of the bears showed any signs of stress or aggression. There was nothing to do but try to relax and enjoy the company of bears.

Mr. Chocolate sat on his bottom like a human, legs outstretched. He pawed at his head, scratching and rubbing. Just to the right of Mr. Chocolate, Wizard was asleep, as was Duffy. Sugarbear lay on her back, picking at herself with gentle nips. My apprehension lifted, because it was obvious that these bears meant me no harm. At this moment, in this place of extraordinary wild beauty, the animals I loved chose to be near me. I brought out a pillow from the tent and rested. We had all worked hard during the day, and deserved a rest. After so many turbulent years, I found it ironic that I was peacefully sleeping next to wild grizzlies.

The following morning I awoke alone. The bears were diligently back on the job of survival, and it was time for me to pack up and leave the G Spot. I said good-bye to each bear present. Wizard, Sugarbear, Mr. Chocolate, and Crate went about their business, ignoring me. In their innocent way, they were teaching me another of earth's lessons: Living complete and in the moment was what mattered. As I looked out over the bears, I knew that we shared a corner of the planet just as it was meant to be.

13

The tranquillity of the G Spot was interrupted by the familiar rumble of Bob's Dehaviland Beaver. He circled twice, then landed in the bay. "Oh, the Lord's given us a heavenly day today, Timothy," Bob said as he spun the tail section about. Bob stopped, squinting in the direction of the fishing bears. "Darn it if that one dark fellow doesn't look like Uncle Chocolate," he said.

"It is Uncle Chocolate—I mean, MR. Chocolate," I said. "This is his second home when he leaves the Grizzly Sanctuary."

"That makes a lot of sense," Bob said. "This place has one of the best salmon runs in Alaska. It's also a pretty short walk from the Grizzly Sanctuary, for a bear. Speaking of the Grizzly Sanctuary, it's time to get you back there for a last visit. All aboard!"

"I don't know if you realize it," Bob said, "but it's the first of September today. Not too many bears stick around this late in the Grizzly Sanctuary. Whatever you do, just be careful of that little devil . . . whatchamacallit . . . uh, Fruitcake."

"Bob, it's Cupcake." It was a good thing that Bob never forgot anything when it came to flying, I thought to myself, because he sure didn't have much success remembering the bears' names.

The Grizzly Sanctuary was only a short distance away, just over a mountain ridge. As soon as we flew into the territory of the Grizzly Sanctuary, we saw the choppy seas tossing high waves up onto the shore. It was far too dangerous to land a plane in the ocean.

"Well, what do you want to do, Timothy?" Bob asked over the headset intercom. "We could return to Uncle Chocolate, or even go back to town."

"How about we give the center creek a look," I said hopefully. "The tide is up, and the waters there are usually calm."

"Roger that!" Bob said. "Let's dip down and give her a look."

The center creek was bloated and looked more like a lagoon than a creek. Better yet, the waters were calm, almost as if inviting the float plane to land. "It doesn't get much easier than that," Bob said. "Let's bring you down home now."

As the plane's pontoons landed in the creek, I caught a glimpse of a small orange creature dashing along the creek's grassy fringe. As we taxied toward the bank, I could see that it was Timmy the Fox, and he looked just a little too excited.

"Well, there may not be many bears, but from the looks of Timmy the Fox, it's not going to be boring," I said and laughed.

"Yeah, maybe I should break my rule and take you to the Forbidden Zone. At least there a guy could get some rest," Bob said.

Between our laughs, six smaller orange puffs materialized behind their excited dad. "Uh-oh," warned Bob, "they look like some serious high voltage."

The Beaver revved and roared its engine. A blast of air from the plane blew my Chicago Bears cap off. Timmy the Fox, seeing the hat as fair game, picked it up in his teeth and ran for the weeds. I sprinted in the direction of Timmy. Several minutes later, I found the cap upside down in the weeds, crushed beneath three of

Timmy's pups. They had grown significantly since I had last seen them, and had lush coats of brilliant reddish orange. To say that they filled the hat was inaccurate. They squished it like a pancake. Timmy stared at me with a pleased grin. He thoroughly enjoyed our game of chase.

"Now, kids, that Bears cap has quite a bit of sentimental value, so I'd like to have it back," I said seriously to the little foxes. "However, I believe I've got a replacement hat that you may borrow."

This wasn't the first or last time that Timmy would rip me off. During my history with Timmy he'd stolen a sponge, gloves, camera lens caps, toilet paper, socks, and a swimming suit. I found a Turner Broadcasting baseball cap and offered it to the foxes. The pups squealed as I lifted my Bears hat from underneath them. One even nipped at my fingers.

"Hey! What's the big idea, you little weenies?!" I yelped. As I retrieved the cap, it was very clear that these were Timmy's kids. A fresh pad of silvery gray poop smeared the inside rim. "Aw, for crying out loud, I'm so glad to be back!"

The three culprits and their dad were promptly joined by the rest of the family, and all hell broke loose as the foxes whizzed around. Rather than being annoyed, I rinsed my cap off and joined the party. Excited, one of the babies peed all over my blue zippered travel bag. In return, I pissed on the entrance of one of the den tunnels. We raced around like maniacs, chasing each other until it started to rain. That's when I remembered that I hadn't set up the tent. The first rule in Alaska is to pitch your tent as soon as possible. My reward for slacking off was a soggy tent, a urine-moistened travel bag, and a stinky cap. It was wonderful to be home.

Since the weather had been so beautiful, the rain shower took me by surprise. In this remote wilderness, nothing should have taken me by surprise. Not weather, the dangers of the terrain, and especially not the bears. With the rain shower past and the tent set up, it was time to get on with the final mission of the expedition. Saying farewell.

Most of the bears were gone now. I knew that some of them had probably migrated elsewhere in search of food. That didn't really matter so much to me. I simply wanted to touch the land where they grazed, slept, played, and loved one more time before I headed back to civilization.

My walk through the Big Green was eerie. I didn't see so much as a single bear. Two months earlier, forty or more would have been average. The sedge grass of the field had turned gold and brown. On the ground, piles of bear scat lay, withered and decayed.

Out of the blue, I saw some familiar faces crossing the field. Holly and her now plump cub, Thumper, hiked in my direction. They seemed very serious, heading from A to Z without stopping for any other letters. They paused about fifty feet from me, giving me a chance to wish them all the best.

"Holly, you look absolutely ravishing in your winter coat," I said. Then I turned to her son. "Little Thumper, I was really worried about you in the beginning of the season. But it looks like you're going to be just fine. You be sure to pay extremely close attention to your mother. I expect to see a healthy yearling next season!"

As they moved on, their eyes seemed to twinkle. They looked especially healthy and content, ready for their long winter's sleep. I was sure that they would be here next year when I returned.

Soon after they left the Big Green, Timmy the Fox joined me. We lay down in the field and watched the clouds drift by. To my surprise, Timmy actually remained still for a bit. "Timmy, in a short time, this place will be buried under frozen snow," I remarked to the fox. "You don't get to hibernate like the bears, do you? It's so much harder for you in the winter. You may be a silly fox, but you're tough and courageous. Please be here next spring!" I said sincerely.

During Expedition '95 I visited four different ecosystems, each with a distinct pattern of bear use. The Grizzly Sanctuary, which had the most bears early in the season, also had the least from August to October because it did not have a strong enough salmon run to support high densities of bears later in the year. Unlike the other ecosystems, the Sanctuary did have a small run of silver salmon, or Coho. The silver salmon spawned in the center creek, where Bob had dropped me off. The creek meandered for about five miles, into the interior of the Sanctuary, a dark, scary place I called the Hinterlands. The few full-time residents still around fished anywhere along those five miles. If I were to find these bears, I'd have to hike through the difficult terrain around the creek and into the Hinterlands.

All of the bears that live in the Sanctuary pass through the interior on their migrational journeys, but some always reside in the Hinterlands. However, the bears of the Hinterlands are not as social as the rest of the bears in the Sanctuary. These animals haven't had much contact because people avoided the region. The grizzlies of the Hinterlands are predators whose diet consists mostly of moose and fish. It is one of the few places in the Grizzly Sanctuary where both bear cubs and the rare human visitors must beware. All that moves in the Hinterlands is food for the animals that live there.

Surrounding the center creek are dark, murky swamps dotted with islands covered by alders. Once you are in the Hinterlands, you lose all sense of direction. Once you are disoriented, you are at the mercy of the hidden grizzlies.

I had gone into the Hinterlands only once before, a few years back. I naively hiked back into the interior near dusk, hoping to see a moose along the banks of the center creek. There were no bears along the creek, and as I walked my feet began to sink into gray mud and the terrain began to change. I noticed that there were no other tracks in the interior, although as it got darker I could hear snaps and crackles that I figured were due to the running water. As I got farther along, the creek seemed to slow, and branched off into the stagnant marshes around the tiny islands.

I hadn't been back here before and the islands intrigued me, so I slogged through the mud toward one of the small clumps of land. I had almost made it to an island when the brush started moving, and I heard the huffs of a brown grizzly. In the fading light, the tangled clumps of alders began to sway and loud jaw pops from an angry bear filled the air. I was up to my hips in mud, the perfect target for a charging grizzly. I tried to withdraw without turning my back on the small island and inviting a charge. The mud dragged at my feet, and with each backward step I could see the form of a bear advancing through the trees.

He snarled but did not chase me; I was almost to the creek and the safety of its banks. Suddenly I fell as the grass under my feet gave way. I was plunged into the dark, oozing mud as a crack opened up, completely swallowing me. I struggled to pull myself to the surface, through the mud. As my head, covered with a gray scum, broke to the top I gasped and thrashed around, trying to open my eyes and pull myself out of the crevice. The motion and my startled cry must have attracted the attention of the island bear, because I could hear more huffs and jaw pops as I groped for solid ground. My arms flailed at the mud like a sputtering propeller. I crawled and swam through the marsh until I reached the banks of the creek. Quickly I followed along the creek, not looking behind me, blindly walking out of the Hinterlands and back to the safety of the Grizzly Sanctuary.

Now, years later, I shuddered at the thought of going back into the Hinterlands. There was a possibility that the morning's low tide would summon the bears still in the interior to the ocean, where I could observe them in plain view. It was an optimum time to fish, and I would be nearby to see the last of the bears. If there weren't many grizzlies in attendance the next day, I decided I would take my chances and brave the Hinterlands.

I was extremely tired that night and went to bed just before ten. A good night's sleep was just what I needed. Unfortunately, Timmy's family had other plans for me. They found my tent much too fascinating to leave alone, and for over two hours, they attacked my home. All I could do was weakly threaten, "Aw, for crying out loud! Someone's going to get a good spanking!" It was, literally, raining foxes. My friends at the Northface corporation could truly be proud: The tent they donated was not only water-proof, but fox resistant as well!

Eventually they let up, leaving me wide awake in the dark. The expedition was about to end. The ways of the wild had become mine, and I wondered if I could readjust to American civilization.

The next morning, Mickey the bear strolled by the tent in tip-top shape. His rear legs, which he had dragged in pain earlier in the season, were in fine working order. He paused directly in front of the tent, curious. Did he remember the tent when it was stationed in the Big Green toward the beginning of the expedition? Would he remember me, and did he know that I had tried to protect him so that he could heal? I sang to him. For each bear, I had a particular rhythm, tune, and tone of voice. Mickey's face beamed as I sang him his special melody. He sat upright on his behind and listened closely.

"Mickey, I'm so pleased to see you strong and healthy! I met another bear in a place called the Forbidden Zone that was hurt just like you were. To tell you the truth, he looked a lot worse than you. Your recovery gives me hope for him. Catch lots of fish today, Mickey. I'll be right there with you all the way."

Mickey picked himself up and slowly moved on. During the conversation, we had looked straight into each other's eyes. There was such a gentle look in his gaze that I was sure he was pleased to see me.

Timmy and Kathleen had returned to investigate the camp without their pups while I prepared my photographic gear. I left a half-drunk can of Coca-Cola unguarded—which was a major error with Timmy the Fox around. With all of my gear in place, I turned and took a healthy swig from the can. "Aw, for crying out loud, Timmy, you pissed in my pop!" I retched and shouted, "What kind of friend are you? Couldn't you have just peed on my tripod or tent, as usual? You have really sunk to an all-time low!"

The fox gazed at me with his big, innocent eyes. "Don't try to play dumb with me, mister! You're wound up like a clock!" Timmy was extra hyper today. Maybe it was the beautiful weather.

I hiked out to the ocean as the tide fell. There were no bears around, so I stripped down to my swimsuit and got a little sun. The warm light felt good, so I relaxed for a while, waiting for the grizzlies.

As the ocean water receded, the flow of the creek became more distinct, creating prime fishing conditions for the bears. Mickey was the first to investigate. I moved a bit closer but made sure to leave a wide margin so as not to spook any of the bears. Though I knew most of the bears of the Grizzly Sanctuary, I had been gone for over a month. New bears who didn't know me might have migrated to these parts.

The next bear that peeked out and boldly pranced over was no stranger. It was Cupcake. Although I was wary, my heart warmed because he was no longer alone. The bear with the Cake was similar to him in size and age. It looked as if Cupcake finally had a playmate. As Cupcake led, his friend caught up and made a half-hearted effort to tackle him. Cupcake responded with a few spirited swats. Then they kissed and preened each other, continuing on to the creek.

Mickey dashed through the water with a speed and skill that made me proud. After sprinting a hundred yards, he thrust his head underwater and emerged with a silver salmon. As Mickey tore apart the fish, a number of other bears proceeded to the creek.

Large bears Hefty, Windy, and Tar strode out separately, while

Holly and baby Thumper waited by the shoreline. A subadult I didn't recognize scampered out in his fluffy golden-brown winter coat. First, he dove into the water, not to fish, but to cool off. The temperature was already well over seventy degrees, which meant that the bears would need to escape from the heat in the cold water.

As the bears jockeyed for position, a pattern took shape. The most dominant bear was Hefty. Even months earlier, when the Grizzly Sanctuary was full of giant bears, Hefty had commanded a decent amount of respect. Only Mr. Chocolate, Garth, Hulk, Warren, and Czar had been higher on the ladder of dominance. With those bears absent, Hefty had no competition. I had a much better relationship with the other big bears, but I could not complain about Hefty. He was even-keeled, though slightly aloof. As Hefty moved, the other bears shifted around the creek. First Tar shifted, which caused the unknown subadult and Mickey to relocate. In turn, that displaced Cupcake and companion, who fled the creek, overacting as they retreated. I named Cupcake's friend Dash, which accurately described his personality. Dash always seemed to be running, either with Cupcake or from another bear. I knew that Cupcake saw me, but he paid me no mind as he thundered by.

Meanwhile, Hefty, the cause of their paranoia, was asleep on the beach as the tide receded. Everyone else slowed down as well because of the heat. Everyone, that is, except for Cupcake and Dash. They kept running until they hit the ocean, where they dove into the water and began wrestling. For Cupcake, life was good. At long last he had found a friend.

A good distance away, another bear loped toward the low tide creek. I zoomed in with my binoculars, and was thrilled. The grizzly was as white as a polar bear, and I only knew of one bear with that coloration: Beacon. After many years, Beacon had safely returned to the Grizzly Sanctuary.

As several of the bears resumed fishing, Timmy put his clown-
ing on hold, hoping to scavenge some fish. A few discarded
salmon would be ample food for him and his family.

Because the Grizzly Sanctuary did not have a heavy salmon run
like the other areas I had visited during the summer, the bears had
to work hard to catch only a few fish. They sprinted, braked, pivoted, and twirled like world-class soccer players at a tournament.
However, a lot of their effort went unrewarded. I hoped that the
run of fish would pick up later in September, when pink and dog
salmon would spawn in the Grizzly Sanctuary.

To rate the best fishermen, all I had to do was watch Timmy.
Each time they caught a fish, he waited nervously for the remains.
Then he ran off the scavenging birds, stole the carcass, and buried
it in the sand a short distance away. After he repeated the process
several times, I realized that Timmy was stockpiling fish for the
family. My theory was confirmed when Kathleen came by, dug up
the fish, and carried it back to the pups, waiting anxiously along
the shoreline. As unruly as they could be, they did not venture out
among the bears. If one excited pup drifted over too far, Kathleen
would bark and yip it back into line. The complexity of the foxes'
behavior and the depth of their intelligence was astounding.
Although Timmy and the foxes could be mischievous and annoying, I really respected their smarts.

Holly and Thumper also patiently waited on the shoreline.
After carefully sizing up the situation, they had decided not to fish
among the tide creek bears. Aside from a few subadults, the area
was dominated by large males. If Holly were to fish successfully,
she would probably have to leave Thumper alone and unprotected.
Thumper was about eight months old, and weighed between sixty
and eighty pounds. Thumper wouldn't stand much of a chance if
one of the males happened to attack. Although none of the fishing
bears appeared aggressive, they were opportunistic omnivores.
Holly computed the variables and thoughtfully withdrew.

Holly wasn't the only one with a problem. Hefty seemed terribly hot and uncomfortable. He solved his dilemma by finding a shallow pool in the low tide's sand. It held just enough cool water to make an excellent bed. He flopped in the pool on his belly, keeping his paw pads submerged in the water to regulate his body temperature. Hefty used his right front limb as a pillow. This kept his head propped up so he could breathe freely as he lay in the cool water. It was so hot out, it was hard to believe that autumn was just a few weeks away. The temperature in the shade was pushing eighty degrees. Then Timmy the Fox came up behind the sleeping bear and took a big, stinky crap. Hefty jerked his head up, staring at Timmy in disgust as the fox danced away. "Heck, Hefty," I said to the annoyed bear, "you got off easy. That darn fox has dumped on my shoes, hat, and tent. He's pissed on or in everything I have in the wilderness. And the worst part is, there are six more just like him."

Suddenly, Cupcake and Dash made a beeline in from the ocean, right at me. I was apprehensive, wondering if the Cake might give me a run for my money now that he had a partner. I backed up, offering the pair clear access along the creek. As they got closer, they slowed noticeably. Dash cowered behind Cupcake's rump, intimidated by my presence. Cupcake remained confident, and stepped toward me. I spoke calmly. "Cake, that's a right fine friend you've got there. I'm very proud of you, and I love you very much." They stared at me and time stood still.

As I looked at Cupcake, I was certain that he was destined to be a giant. At three and a half, he was already pushing 400 pounds, just as big as some of the mother bears. When he reached 1,000 pounds, Cupcake would be a killing machine. A half-ton grizzly that charged humans didn't have good prospects for survival.

The young grizzly looked intently at me. Did he harbor any resentment over our past encounters, or was he just showing off for his friend? Suddenly, a fish cracked to the surface of the creek, just behind them. The pair whirled about, leaped, and crashed into the water, forgetting all about me. Dash emerged with the fish, and Cake wrestled him for possession. In the scrambling, they lost it. But they didn't care, they had each other. That was more than enough.

I crawled into the tent for my last night in the wilderness. Tomorrow I would fold it up and head back to civilization. As I lay in the sleeping bag, I started to get sentimental about my little home. It had sheltered me from the elements, and had provided a safe and unobtrusive home among the grizzlies. On occasion, it was even a haven for Timmy the Fox. I drifted off to sleep, cherishing the sounds of the wild and wishing I could stay.

My last morning was beautiful. By midday the tide had turned, and I drifted among the bears on the beach as if this day would never end. The same bears were in the creek, as if they had never left. For them there was no beginning or end; the Grizzly Sanctuary was their life. I, on the other hand, would depart later in the day. It was time for me to say good-bye.

Mickey fished close by, his hind legs mended perfectly. He had trusted me so much that he convalesced safely near the tent. I had known Mickey nearly all of his life. When he was a young subadult, I had watched him clam tentatively near Booble. Now I was proud to see him fish with such vigor. Mickey and I had a past, present, and, with a little luck, a future.

A little way down the beach was Beacon. Years ago he had been the very first adult male to accept my presence. I truly believe I had saved Beacon's life from the poachers who had landed on the shores of the Grizzly Sanctuary. I had seen him mate with Comet, who gave birth to Saturn, who in turn had her first cub this year, Wilcox: I knew Beacon's family. I hoped that the white bear would be here next season, a great-grandfather of future generations.

Next there was Tar, who I'd also known for most of his life. He'd gotten skunked by Hulk earlier in the year, and lost a girlfriend in Daisy. But I knew that there would be many more romantic chances for such a handsome bear to pass on his genes. I looked forward to knowing his children.

Farther away, Cupcake fished and frolicked with his adopted friend, Dash. I purposely kept my distance so as not to tempt fate. It seemed odd, but in spite of our past difficulties, I may have loved Cupcake the most. I hoped that he would continue to grow and flourish in the kingdom he was destined to rule.

I walked dejectedly back to my tent. It was time to pack it up for the last time. Timmy the Fox and family were all on hand to "assist." For the most part, they did their best to get in the way, or to steal anything they could cart off. After everything was disassembled and organized, I headed up the creek, hoping to find Holly and Thumper. I didn't really want to cross into the Hinterlands, but there was a good chance they were fishing upriver, in the interior. I couldn't bear to leave without saying a final good-bye to them, so I decided to be brave and give the Hinterlands another try.

As I hiked up-country, Timmy yipped in concern, then retreated to his den. I took his warning very seriously, since I knew from past experience that clandestine bears lurked in the interior. I would also make sure to keep my distance from the little islands; I was really beginning to spook myself.

The interior was intimidating and unattractive. It was difficult to maneuver through the alder thickets and the wet and spongy ground. The day was extremely hot, and the 67 million mosquitoes and flies made the trip sheer torture. What was I doing out here in this mess? Why hadn't I respected Timmy the Fox's judgment? That little clown knew everything.

I saw a stretch of land that looked stable and inviting. I hesitantly stepped up to it, wary of the crevices that could open up and swallow me. The day was getting hotter, and a swarm of flies and gnats buzzed around my exposed face. I swatted at them, cursing the Hinterlands. I wasn't watching where I was going, and suddenly I stumbled forward.

I opened my eyes slowly. I had fallen into a shallow pit littered with long, white sticks. Disoriented, I looked around and stifled a muffled cry. I was staring into vacant sockets over rows of dull, yellow teeth in a skull that was cracked and worn with age. I had landed face first in a bear's bed, next to the skeletal remains of its inhabitant.

Dazed, I sat and looked around the carved hole with the giant skeleton in it. I took out my pocket tape measure and measured the skull. The combined length and width was at least thirty inches, making it one of earth's largest grizzlies. I had no way of telling how long it had been there, or why it had died. Was it old age? Had it been injured beyond repair? Had it starved to death within the Hinterlands, or had it been wounded by a human intruder? I would never know the answer.

I picked up the skull, eager to show it to bear experts so more could be learned about it. As I climbed out of the pit I looked back at the other bones, jumbled and incomplete in the absence of the great skull. In the bright light the bones didn't look macabre or frightening, just sad and lonely, the only remaining evidence of a bear's life. Without a second thought, I carefully placed the massive skull back in the carved hole to rest in peace.

Before turning around, I decided to refresh myself with a swim in the creek. The creek's icy waters came from melting snow on mountains and glaciers. During my long stay in the Sanctuary, it had been the source of the fresh water that had kept me alive. As I swam in its waters, a strong sense of appreciation enveloped me. The creek quenched the thirst of all animals in the Sanctuary, including me. It also fed the bears with fish. On my last day of the expedition, it cleansed me as well. The creek was the life's blood of the Grizzly Sanctuary.

The violent rustling of the closest alders snapped me out of my daydream. Something was approaching, shaking dirt loose from the steep banks and into the creek. My swim had attracted the attention of a bear. Undoubtedly, I sounded like spawning salmon splashing about. Could it be one of the dangerous, antisocial bears? I swam to the safety of deeper water, prepared for anything.

First, a large grizzly head craned over the side of the bank for a look. Then, a miniature version popped up on its left side, while another small head appeared to the right. I knew those bears. "Booble! Ginger! Fresca!" I yelled in delight. "It's me, your old pal Timothy. Sorry I'm not a salmon for dinner!" Booble, Ginger, and Fresca sat down and stared at me.

Of all of the bears in my life, Booble was my first true bear friend, the animal who inspired me to live a decent, positive life. All those years ago, when she was only a youngster, I had dedicated myself to her and all of the bears. I pledged never to drink again. I promised to be her friend. I had lived up to the bargain with myself. I wasn't perfect and never would be, but now I was a friend and protector to Booble and all of the bears.

I climbed out of the creek, drying off and singing songs to the bears. They looked healthy and wonderful, and their winter coats were thick and lush, making them ready for their long sleep. Ginger and Fresca would den with Booble this winter, then probably be on their own next year in the Grizzly Sanctuary.

Tearfully, I bade them farewell. It was time for me to leave. As I gathered myself together, I made another pledge to Booble and family. "Booble, the world must know of your ways. I will fight for your survival. One day people will understand and stop destroying your homes and killing your kind. I'll return next year and protect you, Booble."

In a perfect world, the expedition would have ended right then and there. Unfortunately, it isn't a perfect world.

Upon returning to my camp, my exhilaration turned to frustration. Every piece of my carefully packed gear lay strewn about the weeds, as if a bomb had been detonated. Kathleen was busy gnawing holes through a hiking shoe. Timmy himself ran in a circle, draped in a pair of long underwear. It would take more time than I had to clean up, because I already heard Bob's plane approaching. This was going to be embarrassing. Mr. Tough Guy Timothy Treadwell had successfully survived living among grizzly bears, only to get bested by a handful of silly foxes. As I hastily attempted to gather my belongings, the maniacal orange balls stared at me through beautiful almond eyes. I melted like butter.

"Awe, for crying out loud, Timmy!"

Expedition '95 ended as it had begun, with my soaring into the sky aboard Bob's Cessna. Only this time it sailed into the east, away from the brown giants of the Grizzly Sanctuary. Timmy the Fox sprinted along the shoreline in a desperate effort to keep up with the departing float plane. As the Grizzly Sanctuary's form took shape below, Timmy gave up and returned to his mate, Kathleen, and their precious pups. Climbing ever higher, the grizzly's other grand refuges took form: the Maze, the Forbidden Zone, and the G Spot. Places where countless animals and their relatives had been at home for so many thousands of years. For just as long, people have feared and vilified them as dangerous beasts. Yet, the great bears had let me in and had taught me the truth. Bears live in perfect harmony with their environment, while we imperfect humans hold the fate of all living things on earth. We must save them.

Far below, Booble, Holly, and Saturn cared for their families. Snowball, Daisy, Molly, and Sugarbear prepared for motherhood, as Czar, Mr. Chocolate, and Garth peacefully ruled the land. Taffy wrestled with Quick, and at long last, Cupcake had his friend. Wizard was inventing new ways to fish, just as Timmy the Fox created new trouble. Soon the long, hard winter would come, and the bears would be snug in their beds, dreaming of the promise of a new spring.

"Be well," I whispered into the plane's side window. "I'll fight for your freedom. Then I'll return to watch over you, I promise!"

Epilogue

Over a year has gone by since I flew away from the bears after completing Expedition '95. I returned in 1996 with a much more conservative and respectful approach. I backed off from the bears, giving them more room while still offering protection from other people. I was able to safely study the bears, yet not infringe on their quest for survival.

It was never my intention for the book or my life to excite and entice others to follow me into the wild. I've never wanted the book to have the effect that Hemingway's description of running with the bulls had. The purpose of *Among Grizzlies* is to educate people about wild bears and to foster their preservation. It is my fervent hope that people will preserve grizzlies and their wilderness habitat. It is my greatest fear that some people might attempt to copy my past dangerous style of study and become injured or killed.

Left alone and free, grizzly bears are peaceful animals. They have always been willing to share the planet with all animals. Can we learn from them and make a better earth? For the sake of our survival and all other life, we must try.

Endnotes

1. Brown, Gary. *The Great Bear Almanac.* New York: Lyons and Burford, 1993.
2. Highley, Keith. "The American Bear Parts Trade: A State-by-State Analysis." The Humane Society of the United States, April 1996.
3. Bledsoe, Thomas. *Brown Bear Summer.* New York: E.P. Dutton, 1987.
4. Larson A., and M. A. Folk. "Physiology of Hibernating Bears," in *Bears—Their Biology and Management,* edited by M. R. Pelton and G. E. Folk. IUCN publication 40, 1976.
5. Ibid.
6. McPhee, John. *Coming Into the Country.* Farrar, Strauss and Giroux, Inc., 1977.
7. Bledsoe, Thomas. *Brown Bear Summer.* New York: E.P. Dutton, 1987.
8. McNamee, Thomas. *The Grizzly Bear.* New York: Alfred A. Knopf, 1984.
9. Walker, Tom, and Larry Aumiller. *River of Bears.* Stillwater, Minnesota: Voyager Press Inc., 1993.
10. Craighead, Frank C. *Track of the Grizzly.* San Francisco: Sierra Club Books, 1979.
11. Hasler, Arthur D., et al. *The Homing of Salmon.* New York: Underwater Guideposts, 1952.

12. Lentfer, J. W., R. J. Hensel, L. H. Miller, L. P. Glenn, and V. D. Burns. "Remarks on Denning Habits of Alaska Brown Bears," in *Bears—Their Biology and Management,* edited by Stephen Herrero, IUCN Publication n.s. 23, 1972.

13. Brown, Gary. *The Great Bear Almanac.* New York: Lyons and Burford, 1993.

14. Bledsoe, Thomas. *Brown Bear Summer.* New York: E.P. Dutton, 1987.

BIBLIOGRAPHY/
SUGGESTED READING

Bledsoe, Thomas. *Brown Bear Summer.* New York: E.P. Dutton, 1987.

Brown, Gary. *The Great Bear Almanac.* New York: Lyons and Burford, 1993.

Craighead, Frank C. Jr. *Track of the Grizzly.* San Francisco: Sierra Club Books, 1979.

Highley, Keith. "The American Bear Parts Trade: A State-by-State Analysis." The Humane Society of the United States, April 1996.

Murray, John A., editor. *The Great Bear.* Anchorage and Seattle: Alaska Northwest Books, 1992.

Peacock, Doug. *Grizzly Years.* New York: Henry Holt and Company, 1990.

Walker, Tom, and Larry Aumiller. *River of Bears.* Stillwater, Minnesota: Voyager Press Inc., 1993.

ACKNOWLEDGMENTS

Among Grizzlies is a tribute to wild animals and a call for humans to preserve them. Along the way, many wonderful people have believed in this cause and have helped me. Without them, this book and my work would not have been possible. I'd like to thank some of them.

First, my writing partner, Jewel Palovak, and her dad, Ted Endicott, who have been behind me every step of the way.

Next, to Rob Wells and Environment Now, whose generosity has made every bear preservation endeavor a success for me.

Several corporations have donated equipment and services to make my work possible. Each expedition's photographic equipment was donated by John Jonny and Mark Wayne of the Minolta Corporation. I'd like to humbly thank Jill Zilligen, Yvon Chouinard, and all of the kind folks at Patagonia Inc. for clothing me and funding my work. Special thanks to Kim Light and all the people at Tamrac for their contributions throughout the years.

I have been blessed by having a guardian angel to guide me,

Marjorie Quon. Thank you, Marjorie—I try so much harder because of you.

All of my journeys within Alaska were made possible by my beautiful friend Kathleen Parker. As a special tribute, I've named Timmy the Fox's lifelong mate after her. Alaskans Joel Bennett and his wife, Louisa Stoughton, have devoted their lives to the well-being of the earth's animals through film and political action. I am very proud to call them friends.

A gathering of people I call the eco-family have nurtured and guided me along the way. Thankfully, with each passing year, they grow in number and support. Among them is America's greatest eco-warrior, Louisa Wilcox, plus Liz Sutherland of the Sierra Club Legal Defense Fund, and Matt Reid and Emily Williams of the Great Bear Foundation. Another person who is the American grizzly's best friend and defender is Tim Stevens of the Greater Yellowstone Coalition. Tim, thanks for your dedicated service, and also for being my friend.

Each expedition to the land of the grizzly has been aided by equipment and services. They include the Northface, Ruth Donahue of ERA Aviation, Butch Tovsen, Tom Walters, Charlie Hall, and Chaz Glagolich.

My survival in the wild would not have been possible without the care of Captain Bob and the great Bill Sims. Bill and I have different philosophies, yet he helps me nonetheless. Our friendship gives me hope that we can save the bears.

In my winter home of Southern California, many people have consistently helped me. Anne Soble, owner/editor of the *Malibu Surfside News,* was the first person to carry my photos and writing in her publication. Truly, any success can be tracked back to this fine Malibu newspaper. Peter and Sarah Dixon of Broad Beach were the first people to believe that my work had the makings of a book. I am grateful for their guidance.

All of the photographic processing and printing has been handled by three outstanding individuals and their businesses. They are Laura Sokolosky of C.M. Labs, Los Angeles, California, Jay Darrough of the Color House, Burbank, California, and Patty Anderson Patrick at Custom Color in Burbank, California.

Special thanks go to my lifelong friend Manny Vasquez, who advises me and assists with his technological expertise. Also to my great pal Warren Queeney, who has always believed in me and was the first to advise "Be the Bear." No words of thanks could ever express my gratitude to Chris and Ingrid Marshall—their wisdom has been an inspiration.

I am also fortunate enough to have had some contributors who are both friends to the bears and myself. Thank you, Andrea and Ed Eliscu, Winston Chen, and Hall Wendall.

I am also extremely grateful to my agent, Carol McCleary, our editor, Eamon Dolan, and his assistant, Sarah Polen.

I'd also like to thank Lyndon Stambler of *People Magazine*, whose excellent feature about my work led directly to this book from HarperCollins.

In conclusion, the bulk of my proceeds from this book will go to the preservation of grizzly bears worldwide.

Jewel Palovak's Acknowledgments

I want to thank Timothy Treadwell, the best friend I've ever had, my mother, Rose, who raised me right, Ted, who is my champion, Shelby, who's always been there for me, Jannis, Margaret, Mario, and all of my friends at Granita Restaurant, and Dr. Brandi Jackson-Davis, who helped me expand my world.

TIMOTHY TREADWELL died in the field with the bears he loved, but his legacy lives on. Jewel Palovak is now at the helm of Grizzly People (a 501c3), the nonprofit organization that Timothy founded. This year, she co-executive produced *Grizzly Man,* a Werner Herzog film. Grizzly Man chronicles the life of Timothy Treadwell, showcasing his passion and unique beliefs. To learn more about bears, preservation, and Timothy Treadwell, visit www.grizzlypeople.com.

Printed in the United States
by Baker & Taylor Publisher Services